Sketching In An Urban Forest

by

Subhash BATHÉ

First Edition

This book is dedicated to:

All the wonderful, resolute walkers of

Taljai Forest Reserve.

My friends, may your numbers never dwindle.

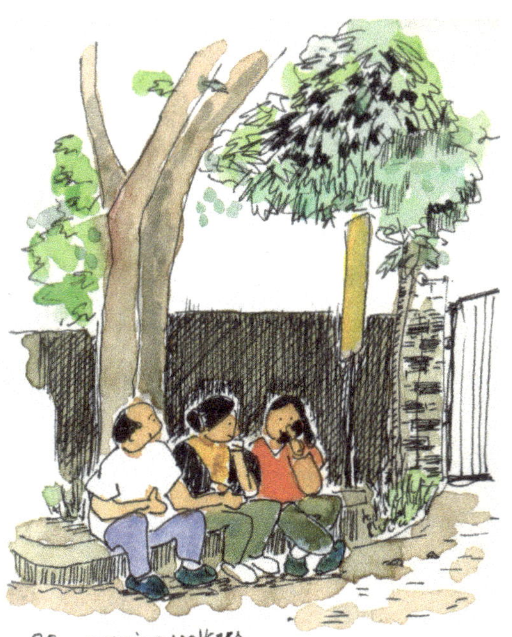

FOREWORD

When Subhash BATHÉ expressed his idea of authoring a book, with very few books being written on urban sketching in India, I encouraged him to take up sketching as his subject.

Sketching as a medium of communication was born before mankind invented language. In this book, the way Subhash has effectively showcased sketching as a powerful practice to communicate daily observations, it will definitely inspire many others to do so.

This book on Taljai forest takes us on a beautiful journey through Subhash's numerous daily walks, expressed through lively sketches and evocative writing. Subhash has managed to combine exercise and sketching perfectly since one activity is all about increasing the pulse rate and the other being the exact opposite is about relaxing and meditating. All sketches are very spontaneous looking, being a result of direct observations in daily life. The various subjects of sketching articulately capture everyday routine activities of humans as well as animals and birds, forming a visual story. Even seasonal changes in nature and human attire are highlighted beautifully.

This book is a great collection of visuals and prose and will surely appeal to both visual artists and avid readers. I hope this book reaches many art enthusiasts and nudges them to inculcate sketching in their daily routine. I congratulate Subhash for crafting this beautiful book. Looking forward to many more.

Ar. Sanjeev Joshi
Architect and Founder-Urban Sketchers, Pune

FOREWORD

The Taljai forest in Pune has been very beautifully penned down, both in prose and sketches, by devoted environmentalist Subhash BATHÉ in his book- Sketching in an Urban Forest.

He has very beautifully and aptly sketched some locations and his observation of flora and fauna is reflected in his poetic description of birds, especially the peacocks as also the other denizens who wander there. Pune's forest greenery is made alive through his expressions.

I appreciate his efforts and wish that his message reaches to all concerned citizens and the abundant potential of future forests is realised, so that not only one Taljai forest, but other hillocks are also converted to forests for the health of future generations. And that more people come out and enjoy themselves in such beautiful surroundings.

I congratulate Subhash for his book and wish his inspiration gets converted into a movement.

Dr. Vinaybala Mehta
Former Principal SNDT College, Former President IFUWA,
Philanthropist, and 3-time Fulbright Scholar

Author's Note

The idea of authoring a book was in my mind for a while and I had started on my first book 'How to become an Urban Sketcher,' which is still half done. Thankfully, this book, 'Sketching in an Urban Forest' is complete. I am happy.

I hope this serves as inspiration to more of my urban sketcher friends, Urban Sketchers Pune (USP) members and others to author their own books and publish them. It gives great satisfaction to see the book in its print form.

Now that I have this book out, there are more in the pipeline, and I hope you and other readers enjoy them too.

Subhash BATHÉ

CONTENTS

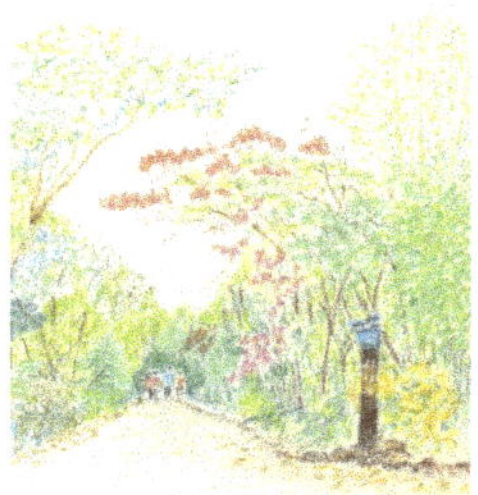
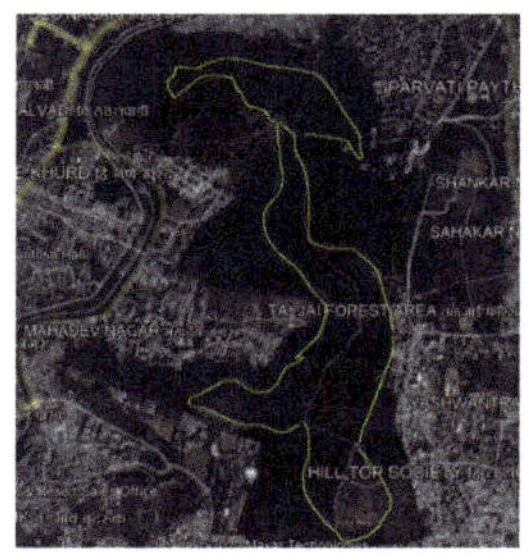
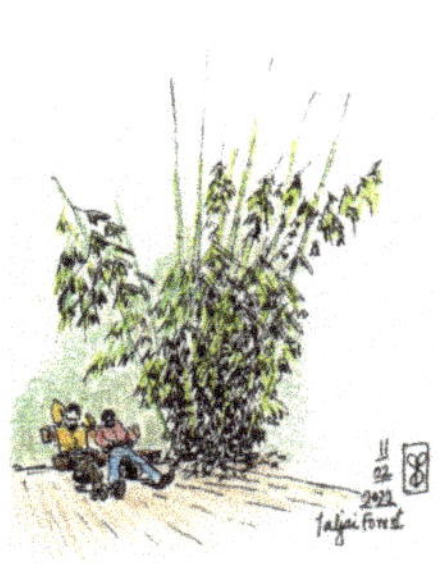

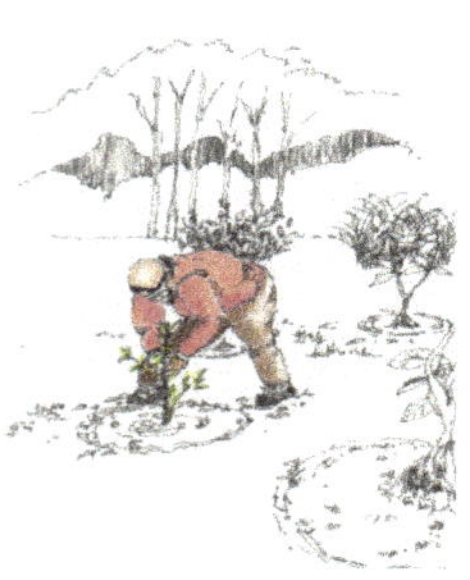
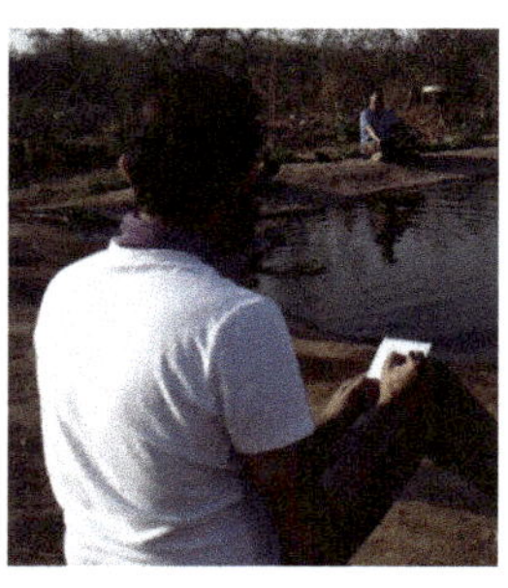
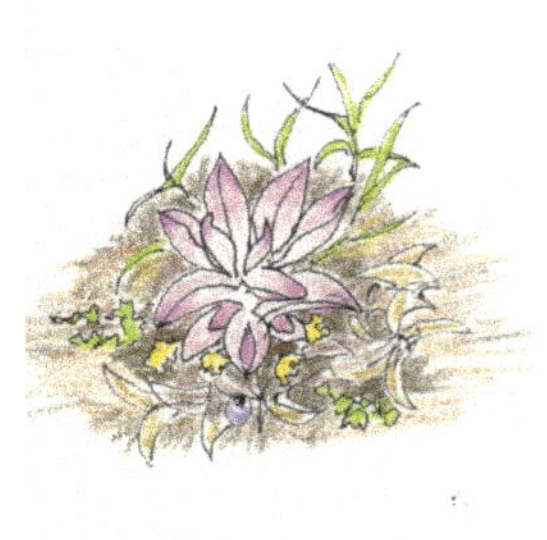

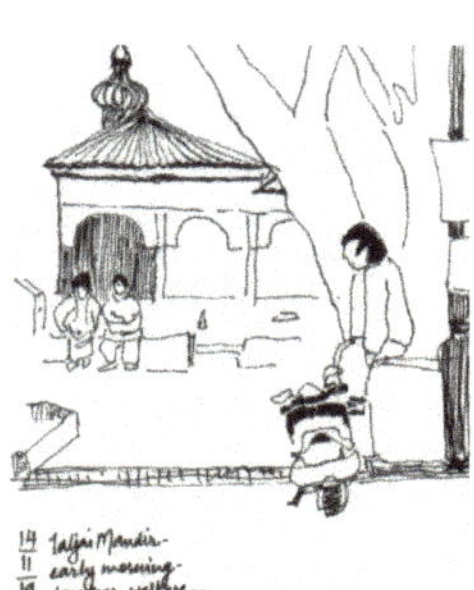
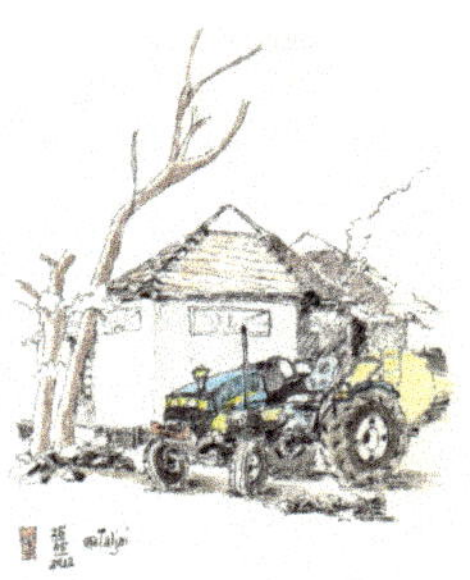
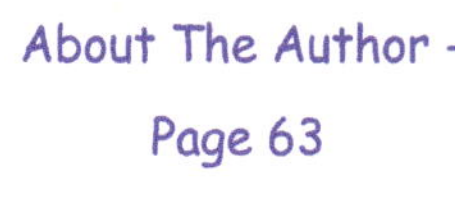

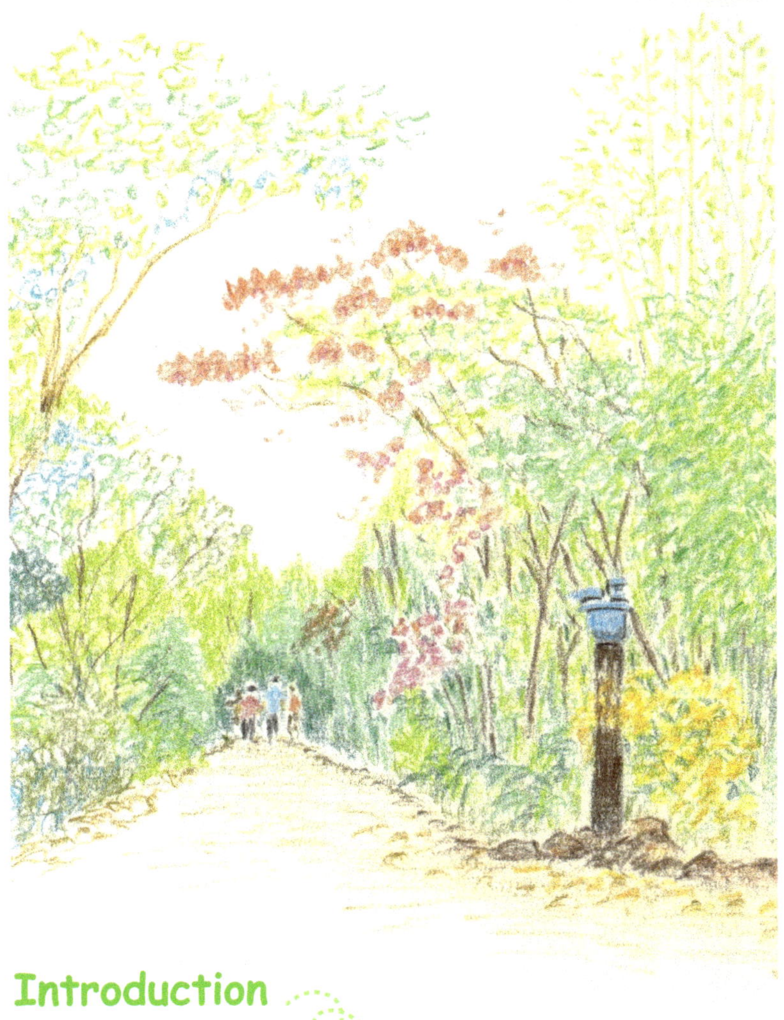

Introduction

Welcome, dear reader. This is a book of sketches, pictures, and stories of an urban forest, in Pune, India. The Taljai forest sits in the middle of a bustling metropolis of seven million people. It is a wonderful place for walks, where we see (and hear) many beautiful insects, birds and animals and witness the mood of the forest changing with the seasons. You may have just such a forest or neck of woods close to where you live and which you perhaps enjoy visiting.

The official name of the forest reserve is Parvati-Panchgaon Vana-Vihar, loosely translated as the forest reserve of Parvati and the five villages nearby. It is popularly referred to as the Taljai forest due to its proximity to the Taljai Mata Devi Temple.

The forest reserve is fenced, and the Maharashtra Forest Department (MahaForest) has been actively planting native trees, arranging for their care, and creating small waterbodies for birds and small animals to drink from. There are benches within the forest to sit down and enjoy nature, the bird calls and simply the solitude. If you are more inclined to physical exertion, there are ample trails for running and walking, in the forest. Similarly, it is a wonderful place for workouts, calisthenics, yoga, etc. Some people come for the easy camaraderie and catching up on gossip. You can experience one or more of these distinct aspects of the forest each time you visit there. This forest offers nature, and the outdoors in a reasonably tame setting. The experience is something that you would like.

For the regulars here, the book will provide a good reference of the wonderful views, interactions, and experiences of the forest while for the newbies, this work will be a collection of information on what they can expect to find and enjoy at this forest or look for in their own favorite forest.

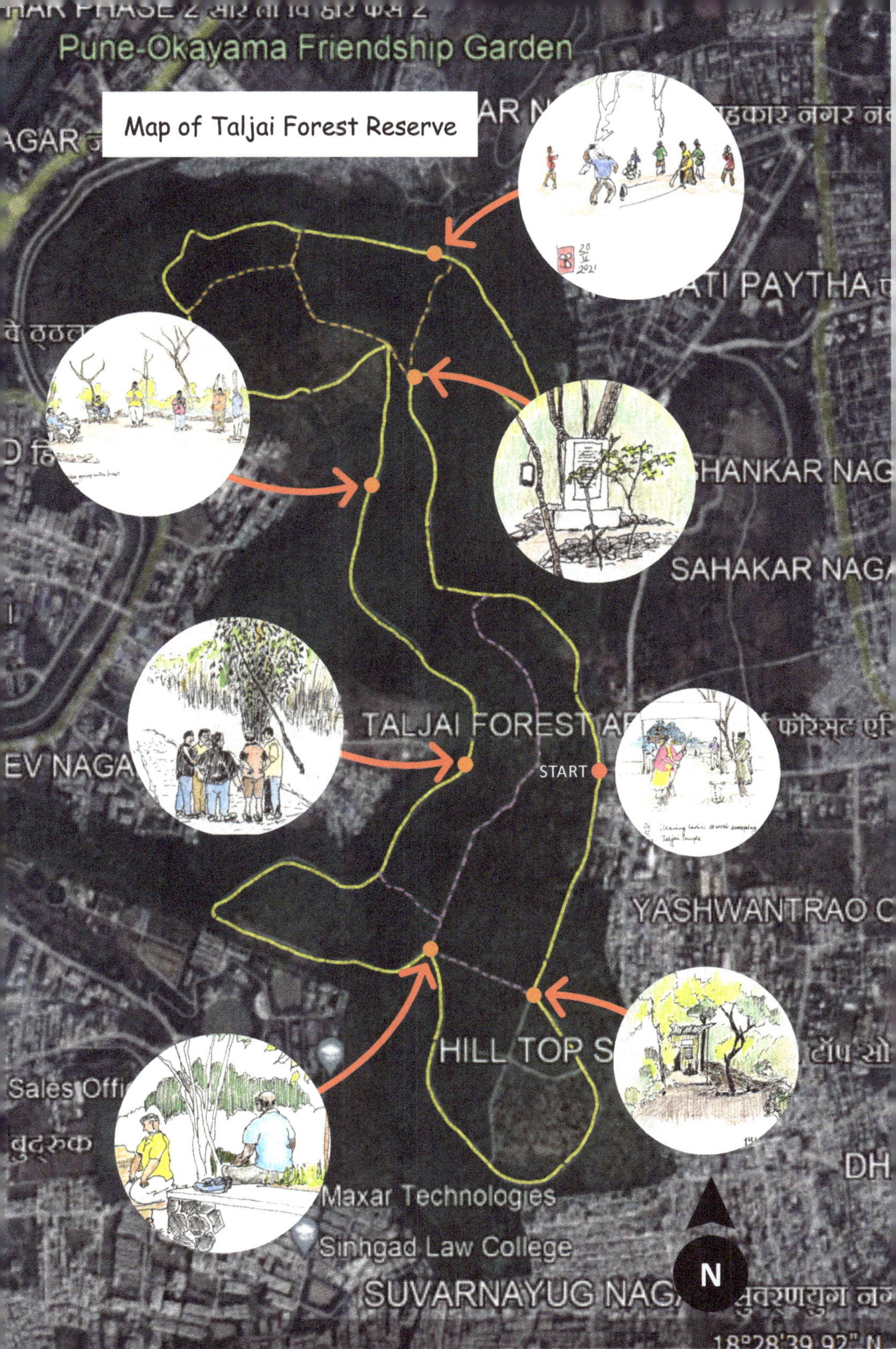
Pune-Okayama Friendship Garden
Map of Taljai Forest Reserve
GHANKAR NAG
SAHAKAR NAGA
TALJAI FOREST AR
START
EV NAGA
YASHWANTRAO C
HILL TOP S
Sales Offi
Maxar Technologies
Sinhgad Law College
SUVARNAYUG NAG
N

Walk Through The Forest

"T6", (short for Taljai @6am) pings the text message each morning, alerting me that my walking buddies are up and getting ready to roll. Whatever brief bout of lethargy that holds me to my bed evaporates and I am up and about.

The thought of the clean fresh air, many bird-calls, and lovely vistas hasten my pace, as I get ready for the walk.

I hop into my car for a short drive from my place to the forest reserve. Even at 5.30 am, Pune is bustling with workers going or returning from their shifts at automobile, electronics, and IT industries. Early morning travelers and the many long-distance buses crowd my route to the forest.

The groceries and fresh produce carriers are zipping around, as are the milkmen, newspaper boys, and the army of cleaners. I know that my morning dose of fresh fruit and coffee will be waiting for me when I get back home.

As I thread my way through the traffic and reach the base of the hill, a different kind of rush slows my drive up the winding road leading up the hill. Early morning walkers, some of them are already returning home, having started their walks at 4 am. Walkers, runners, sportspeople practicing uphill running and cycling, now crowd the road and make it a slow drive up. Though Pune is a noisy city with traffic horns used profusely, it does not feel nice to disturb the early morning quiet and so I cautiously thread my way through all the people and vehicles to find a parking spot near the gate.

Walking along the road, I pass the temple gate and bow quickly to the deity, before hurrying up the slope to the forest gate. I hear greetings and good morning from many friends and respond happily.

I pass the tea stall, doing brisk business so early in the morning. Much of his business is done during the early morning hours. Stray dogs scamper up for a quick greeting. They are great therapists.

When traffic delays my buddies, I whip out my small sketchbook and start sketching. Each of my sketches take a few minutes and that keeps me busy till they arrive. I remember how impatient I used to get earlier. But that was before I started sketching. Now, any opportunity to sketch is welcome.

My buddies arrive and we walk through the gate into the forest. We turn left and that takes us along the border wall, which has been erected to prevent the ever-growing encroachments into the forest, by dwelling houses. Despite that, we see several breaches and houses spilling into the forest reserve. There is no end to man's greed.

We walk along the pathway, under the tunnel formed by tree branches, which cut off even the moonlight that illuminates the forest at this time of the morning. Flashlights are sometimes needed, to avoid stumbling. The wall veers away to the left as the path leads deeper into

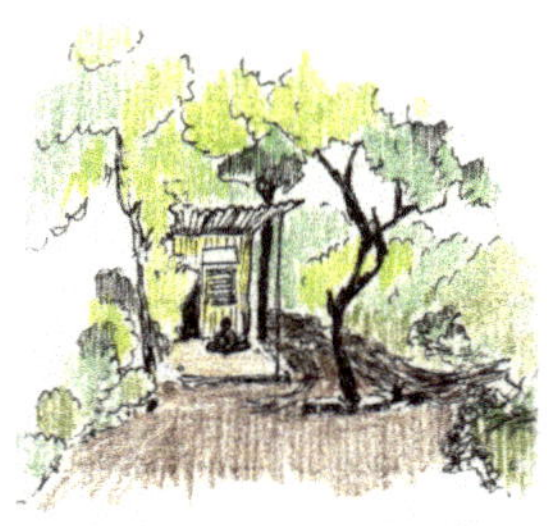

the forest for a while and we come in sight of the first of the junction of pathways on this route. We exchange greetings with some of the regulars who have already reached there and are occupying the several benches around the square. The small forest keepers hut becomes the impromptu yoga place for some intrepid souls.

Walking through the darkness, smells of the various trees and other vegetation damp from the morning dew, fill our every breath. Bird sounds, creaking branches, and snatches of conversations from afar are clearly heard in the stillness. We sense scurrying shapes and rustling in the undergrowth as nocturnal animals move away from people on the pathways.

If we are a bit late and the sun is up, we can see the new gardens that are being created along the pathway. One is exclusively for diverse types of bamboo plants, the other with beautiful arrangements of colorful flowering plants, is for butterflies.

The rising sun starts illuminating the eastern sky. At first, we see only the illuminated edges of clouds high up and a little later, the soft orange glow through the trees, which rapidly turns to gold as the sun rises above the horizon. Quite often, we halt a while to watch this glorious transformation as it unfolds. Soft breeze caresses us as we drink in this scene. Sometimes, the sky turns so red, that it appears for a moment that there is a forest fire in that direction.

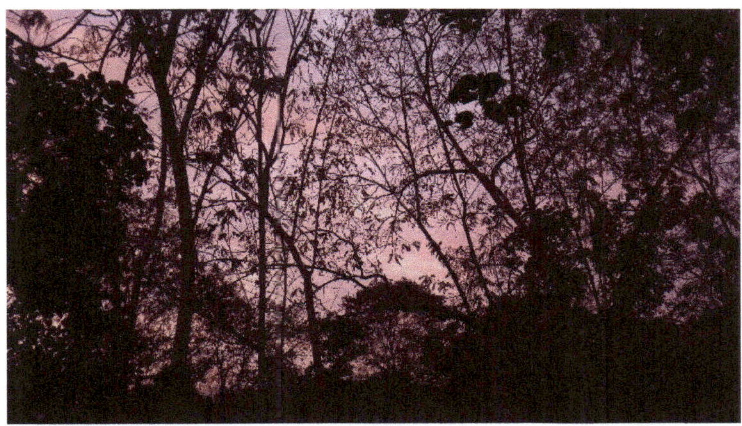

As we move through the forest, we see different trees and some of them are usually flowering as per the season, adding to the beauty of the landscape. Peacocks call out from branches high up in the trees, where they keep watch for their mates feeding on the ground below.

During the months from June to December, the males carry their long plumage which looks impressive even when closed and we see the same birds on their favorite perches often.

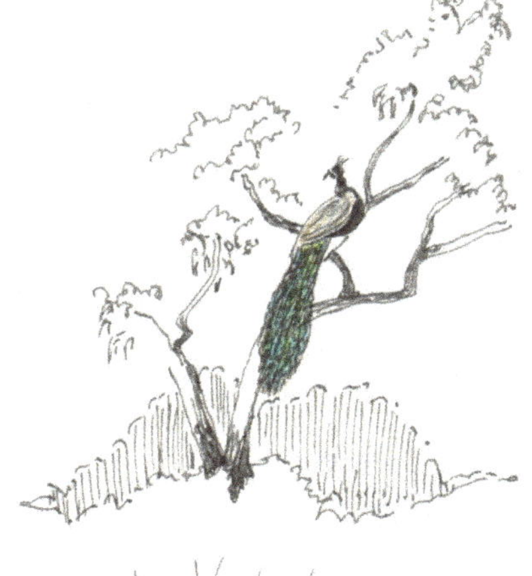

The rainy season from June to Sept is also their mating season here and many a times we get to see the male strutting his stuff, the plumage fully opened into a glorious fan behind him, trying to impress the many peahens who studiously ignore him and go on feeding as if nothing was happening. Must be a tough task impressing those chicks, for we see these guys dance about for quite a while.

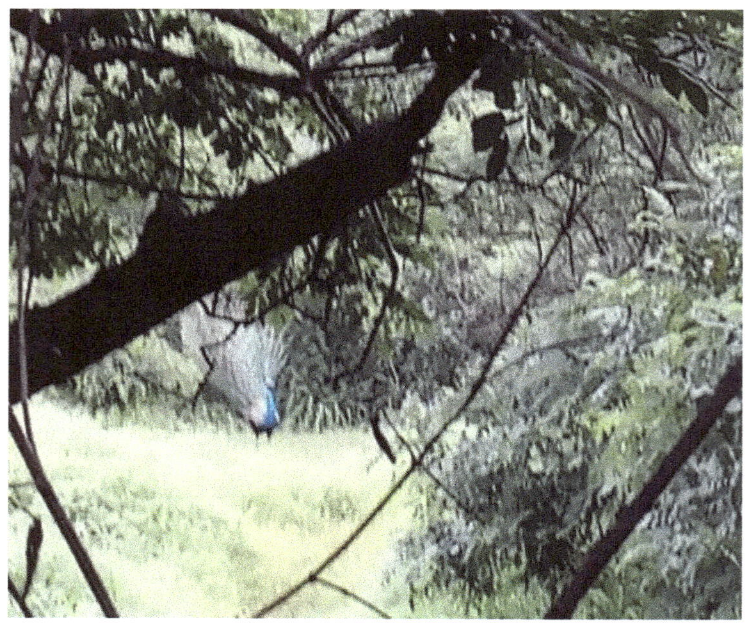

What is interesting is that if you are close enough, you can hear the feathers vibrate as the peacock dances, and this creates a peculiar rustling sound. The sight is quite impressive.

The path loops around skirting the boundary wall again and we have reached the second of junctions on this path. MahaForest has arranged benches around this junction, with a large platform in the middle, which will eventually have a large tree growing from the centre of it. This will mimic the village meeting points under large trees in the village, where

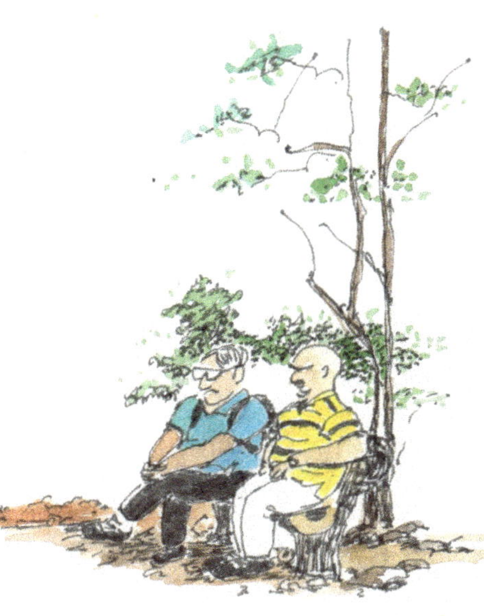

everyone gathers for exchanging gossip and news.

We can see some people practicing their yoga here and others enjoying the beauty of the forest and having conversations with their friends and passersby.

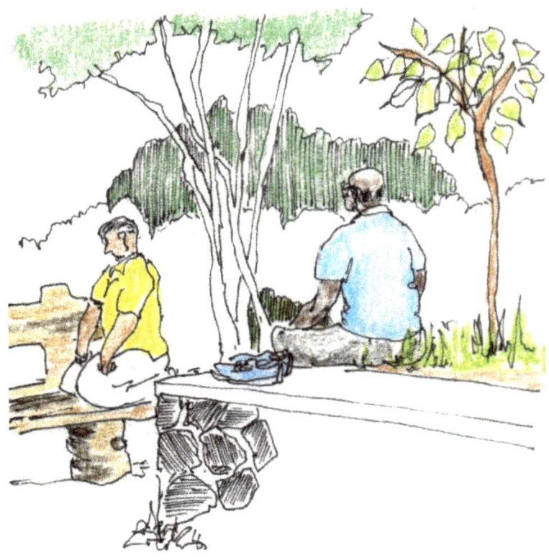

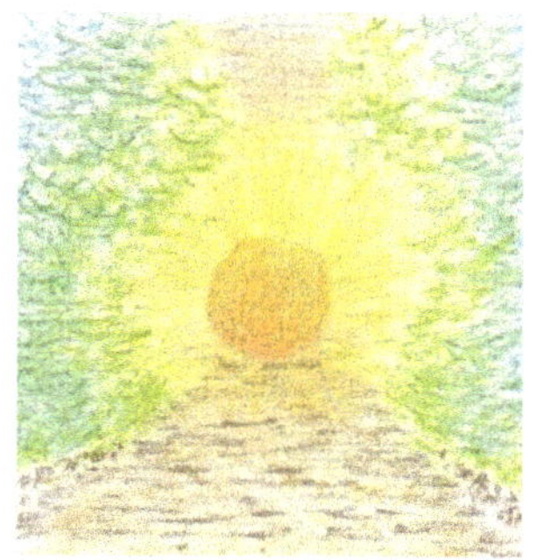

There is a short-cut from the first junction to this one and stragglers from our group use it to catch-up with us, when they are late. The interesting part of this short-cut is that the path is so aligned, that when walking up on this path at sunrise during the winter month, we saw the sun, sitting like a big ball of molten gold, right in the middle of the path. It was an amazing sight, and one to be cherished.

As we cross the junction and take the pathway to the left, the road slopes downhill. One of our buddies is heavy, so gravity and momentum take him downhill in a flurry of rapidly moving arms and legs. Of course, he lags when walking up hill. As the ground levels out, we can see part of the boundary wall, which has a college next door, and we can hear the bustle of the students and smells from the canteen as we walk past.

Further down, we take the lower road, along the western boundary wall. In the summer season, we can see in the distance, the hilltop crowned in crimson by gulmohar trees in full bloom. The path weaves up and down along the hills, giving us our cardio very day.

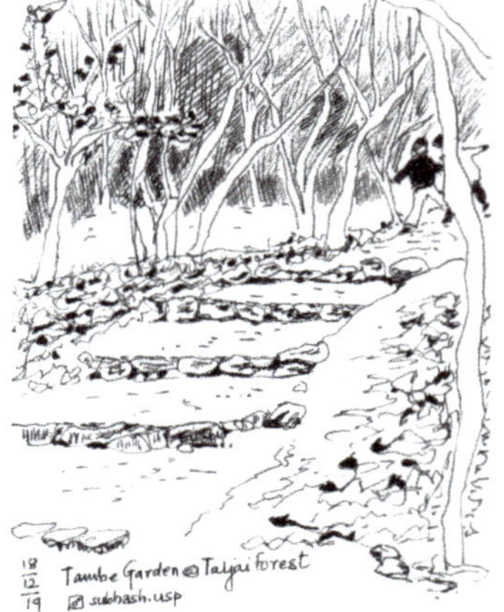

Tambe Garden @ Taljai forest
@ subhash.usp

15

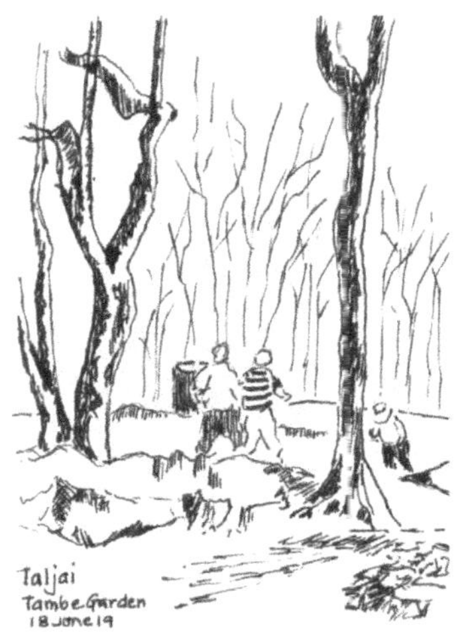

The road rises again and splits in two, one going further along the boundary for a longer track and the other looping back to the entrance gate. People of all ages can be seen working out in this area. There are many attractive places to practice yoga or simply meditate amongst the trees. The sounds of the city fade into the distance and bird calls and the forest noises caress you with the breeze. We have worked up a sweat by the time we reach back near the gate, and we stop to rest a bit on one of the many benches lining the pathway. Some stretching exercises and we are ready to leave. The walk has been good, and I feel the endorphins active already.

Forest walking is becoming quite popular nowadays. I am glad that we have been enjoying this for the past several decades. Indeed, we have been extraordinarily fortunate to be able to live in Pune, which is a large, crowded city and yet be inside a lovely forest within 15 mins. Must have some good karma!

In the following chapters, you will find more of the sketches from my Taljai walks and related anecdotes. You will also notice that some sketches are better than others. These reflect the time I had to sketch them and my sketching journey. I hope you find them enjoyable.

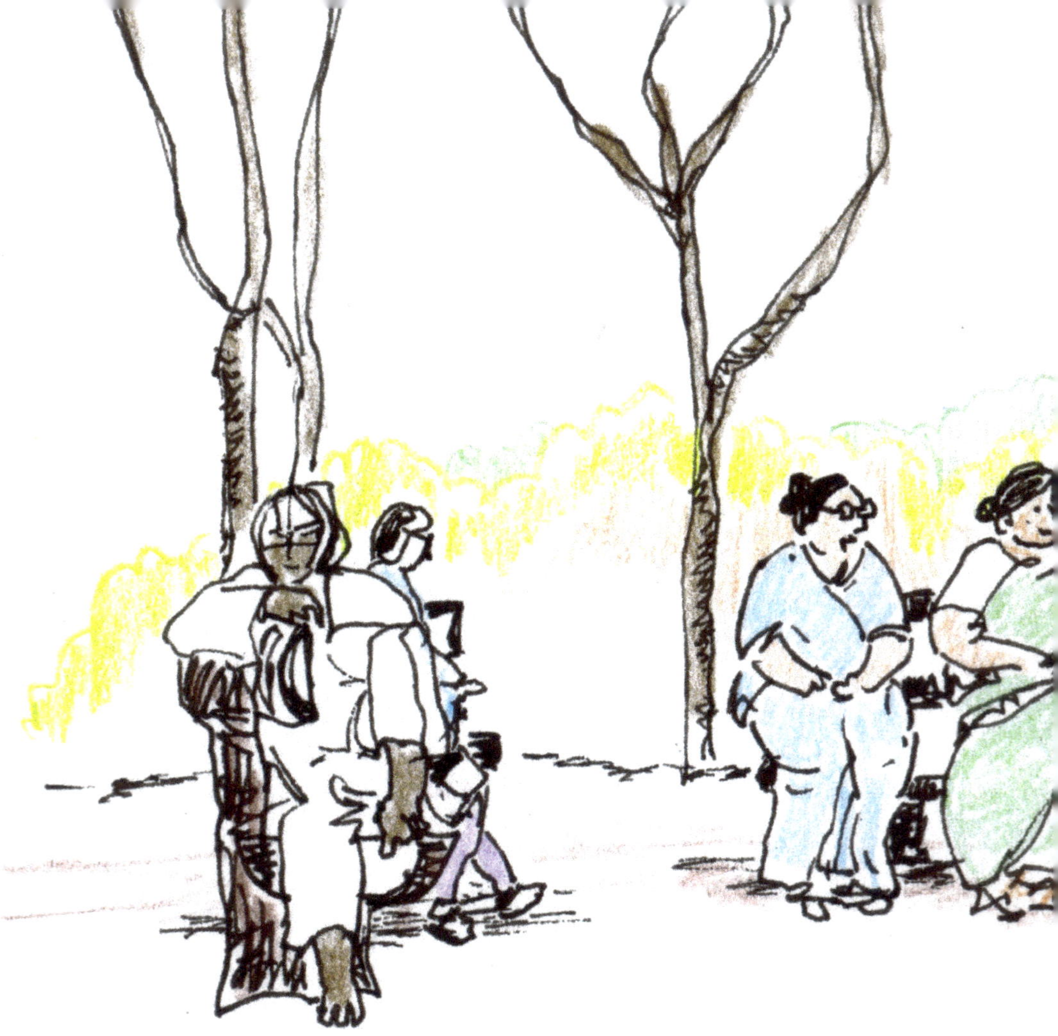

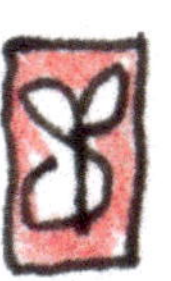

Relaxed conversations
@Taljai

31/05/2022

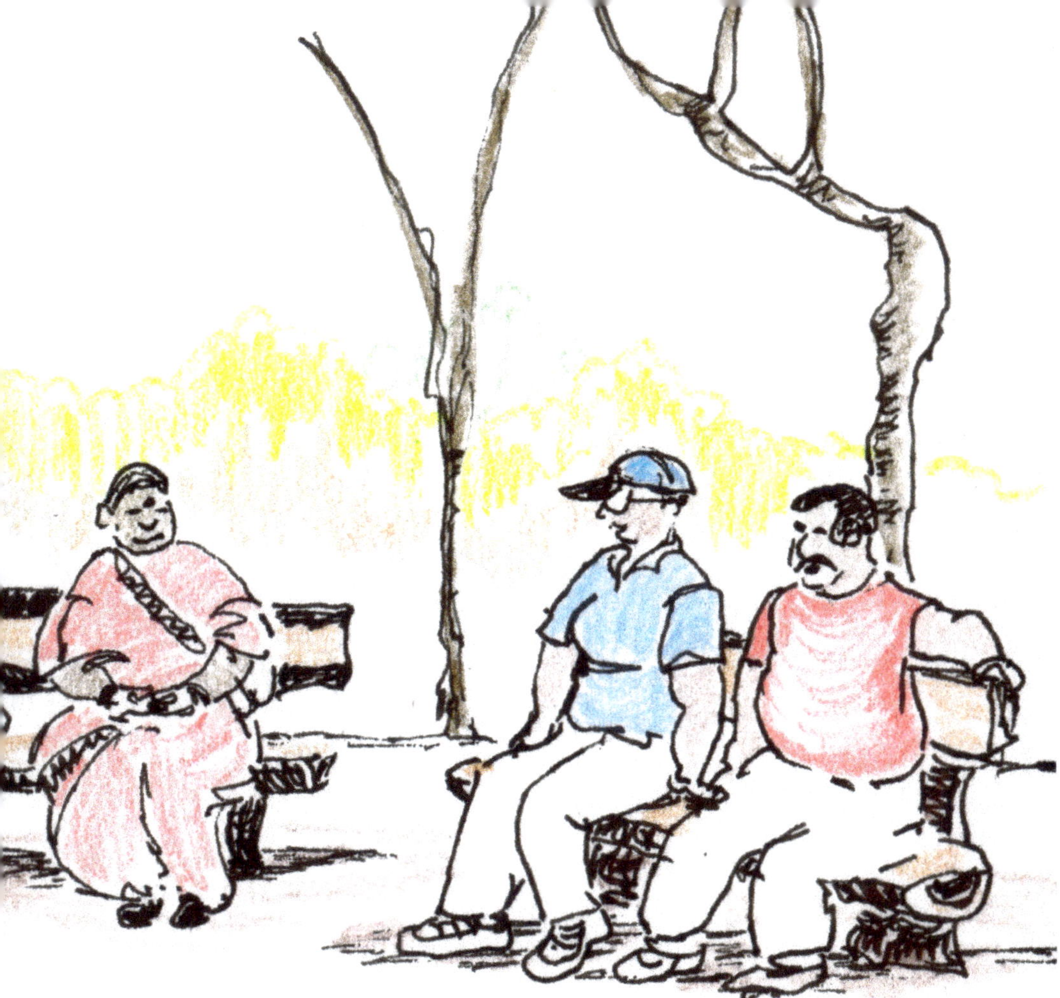

Relaxing In The Forest

Relaxed conversations are a big part of our morning walks in the forest, and we see many people in small and large groups indulging in this favorite past time. It is the ultimate de-stressor. Bad for the shrinks, but particularly good for the people.

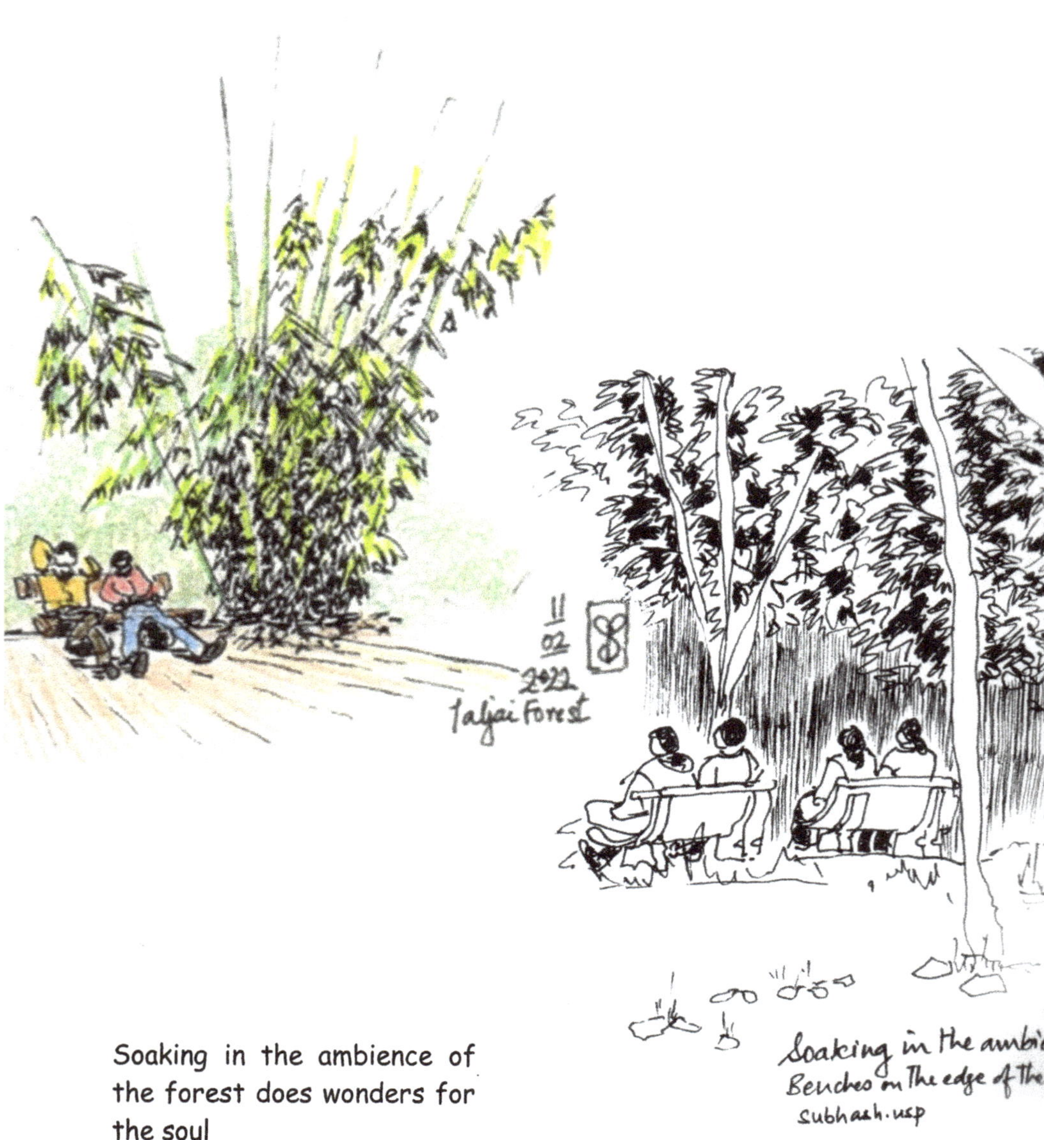

Soaking in the ambience of
the forest does wonders for
the soul

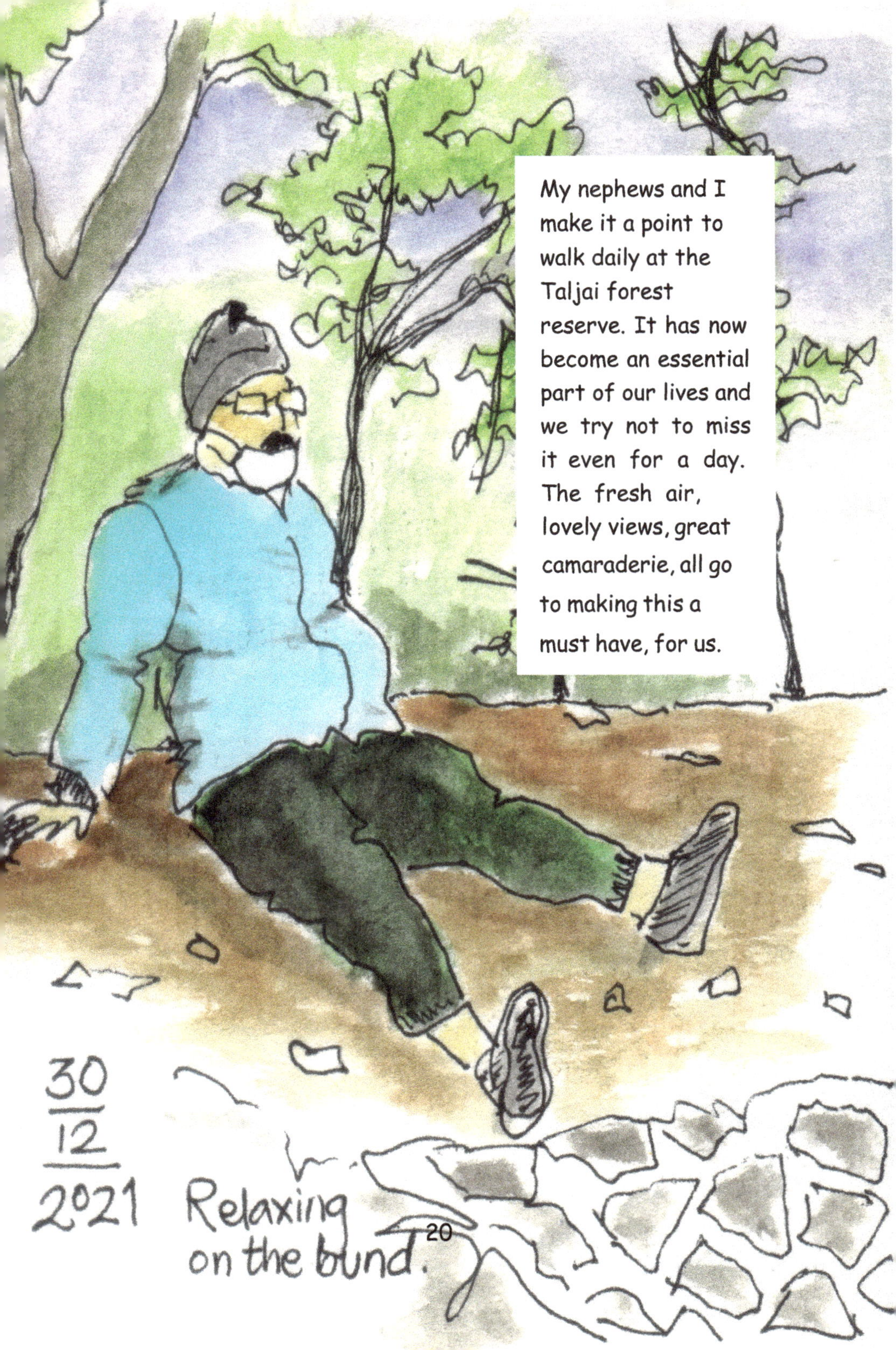

My nephews and I make it a point to walk daily at the Taljai forest reserve. It has now become an essential part of our lives and we try not to miss it even for a day. The fresh air, lovely views, great camaraderie, all go to making this a must have, for us.

30
12
2021
Relaxing on the bund.

20

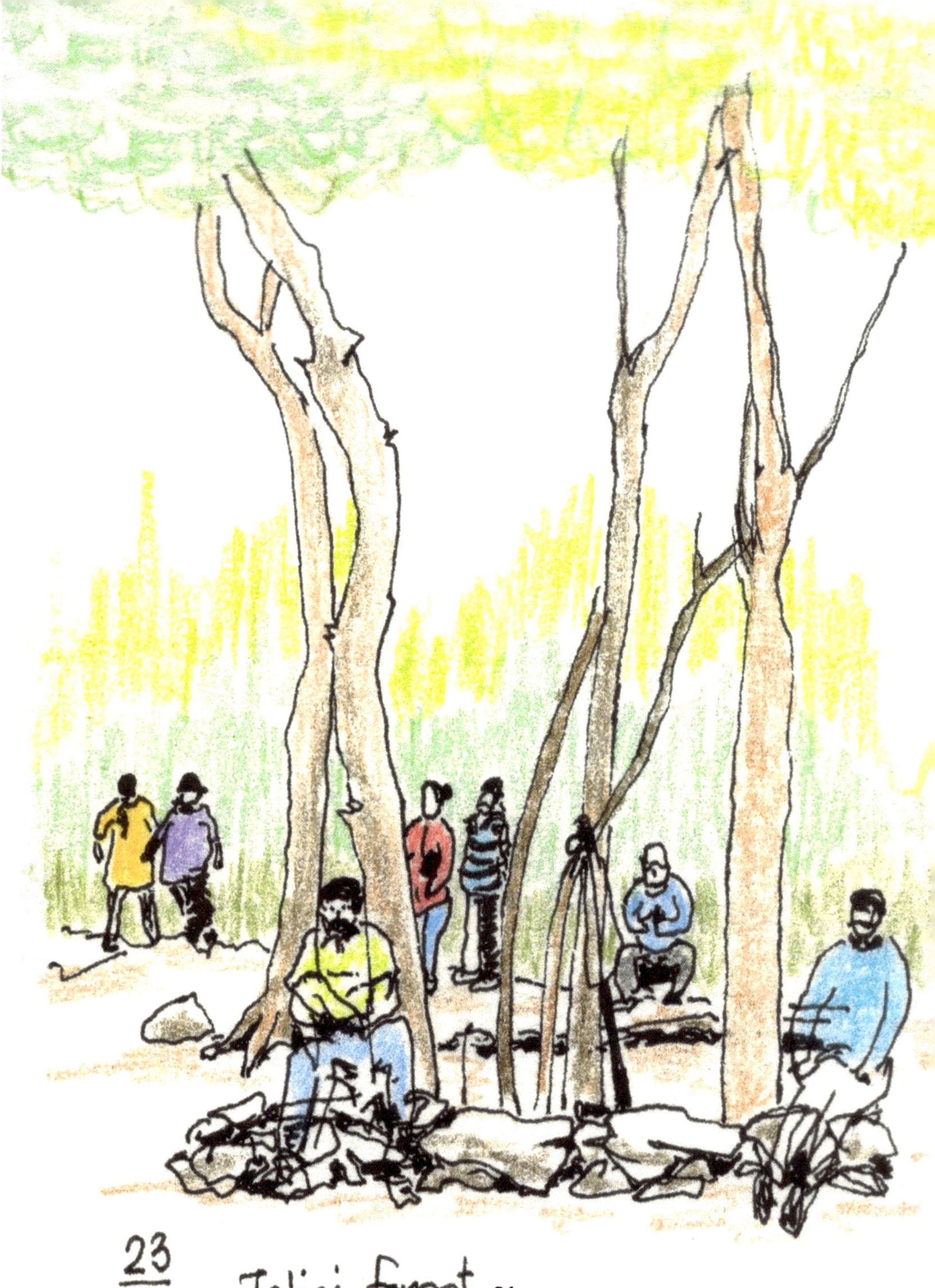

$\dfrac{23}{\dfrac{02}{2022}}$ Taljai forest 21

There are of course the people who stay connected with their tech devices while sitting in the forest and enjoying the beautiful, relaxing environment.

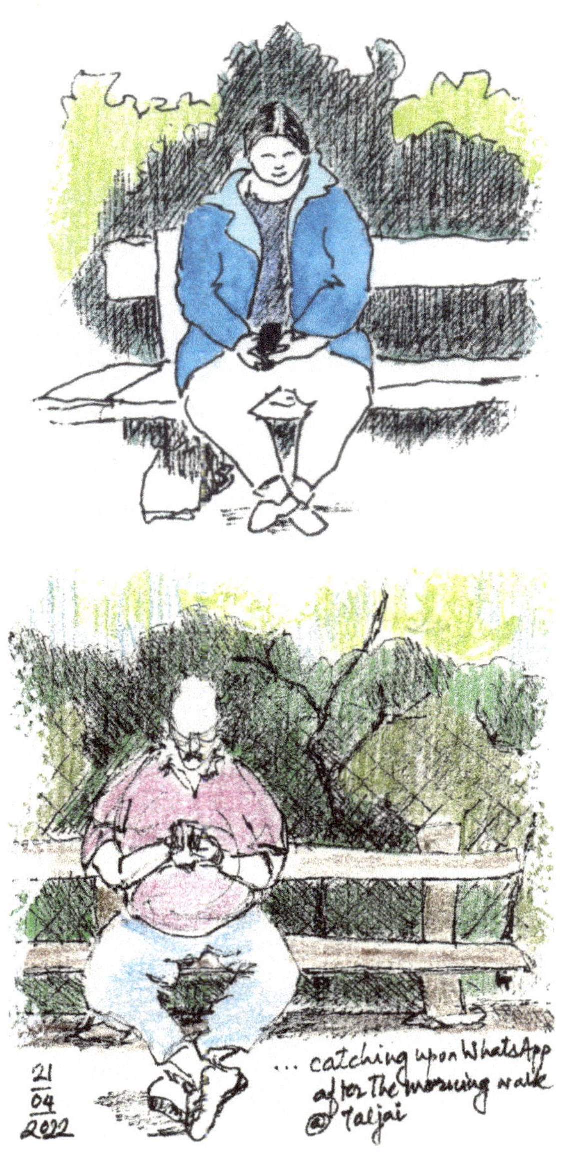

Citizen Initiatives

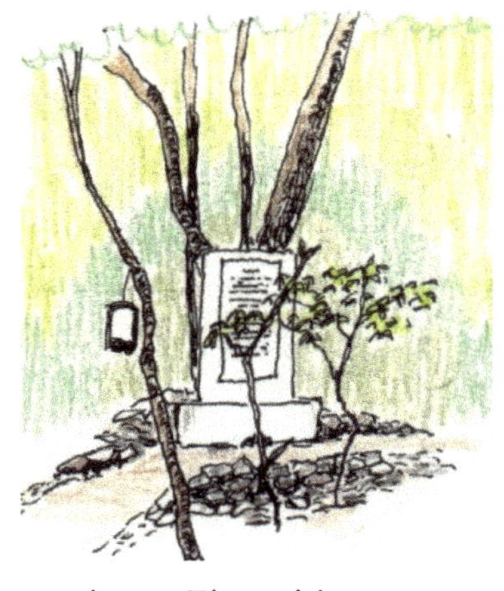

Some very enthusiastic regulars have taken earnest efforts to improve the forest reserve. They have cleared some areas, planted trees themselves, beautified the place by creating gardens. The elder amongst them is Mr.P.S. Tambe, a retired banker, a naturalist, an artist, and a poet. He is an amazing person and a good friend of mine.

In the middle of the forest there is a poem carved in stone, which has been written by him. The poem, loosely translated reads -

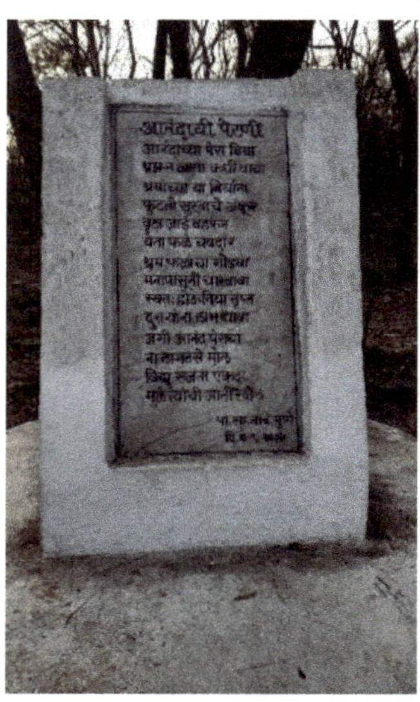

Plant Happiness- P.S. Tambe
Plant seeds of happiness, your efforts will not be in vain
From your efforts will sprout leaves of joy
The tree will flourish and there will be tasty fruits to enjoy.
Enjoy fully these fruits of your efforts and share too the joy.
It costs you nothing to plant these seeds of joy, for once they take root, they will go deep and spread the joy.

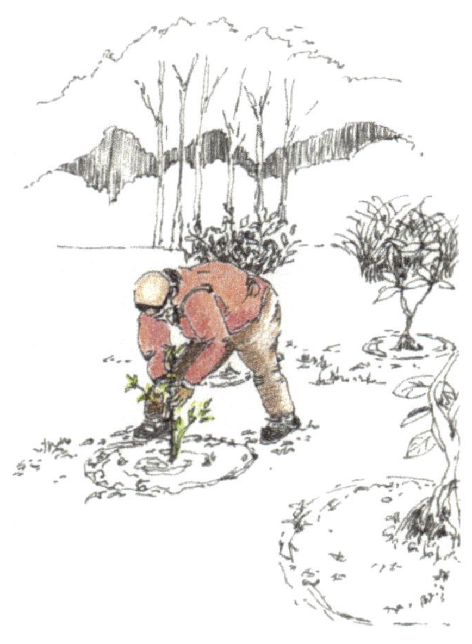

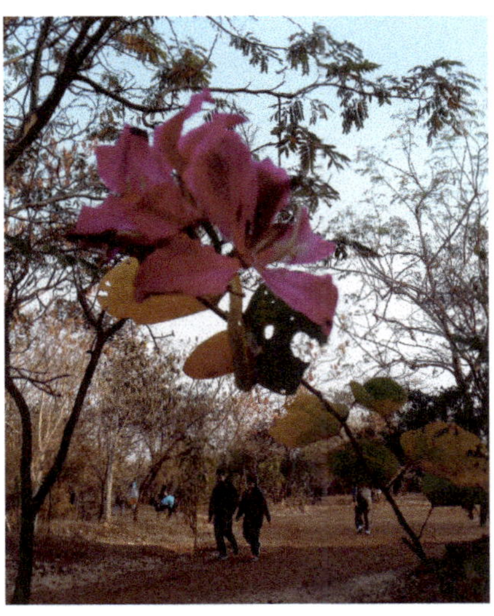

Another person we meet often is Ajay, with his tradmark red jersey and goggles perched on top of his clean-shaven head, who diligently nurtures fruit trees and protects the wildlife in that area.

One can clearly see his love for the trees and the forest in the way he assiduously nurtures them and cares for the birds and animals that live there. He has shown us several types of nests, newly laid eggs of various birds, baby snakes, etc. and speaks knowledgeably about the various native species that inhabit the forest.

Sketching In The Forest

Since I took up sketching in 2019, I have been trying to learn how to draw better. I started carrying a small sketchbook and pen with me on my walks.

Many of my sketches were made, while waiting for my walking buddies to join at the start or while in the forest, when something caught my eye, and I could immediately capture that in a sketch.

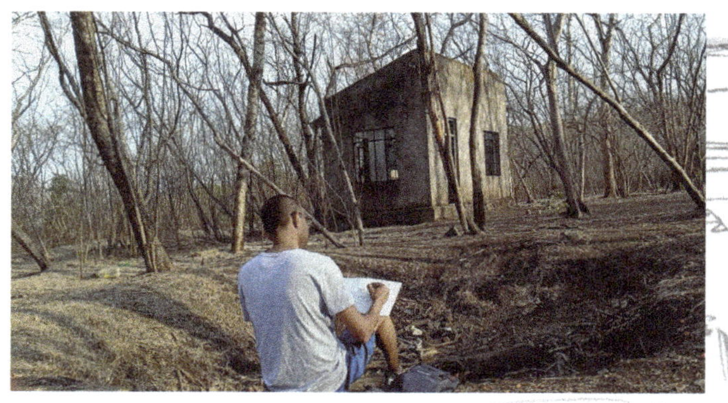

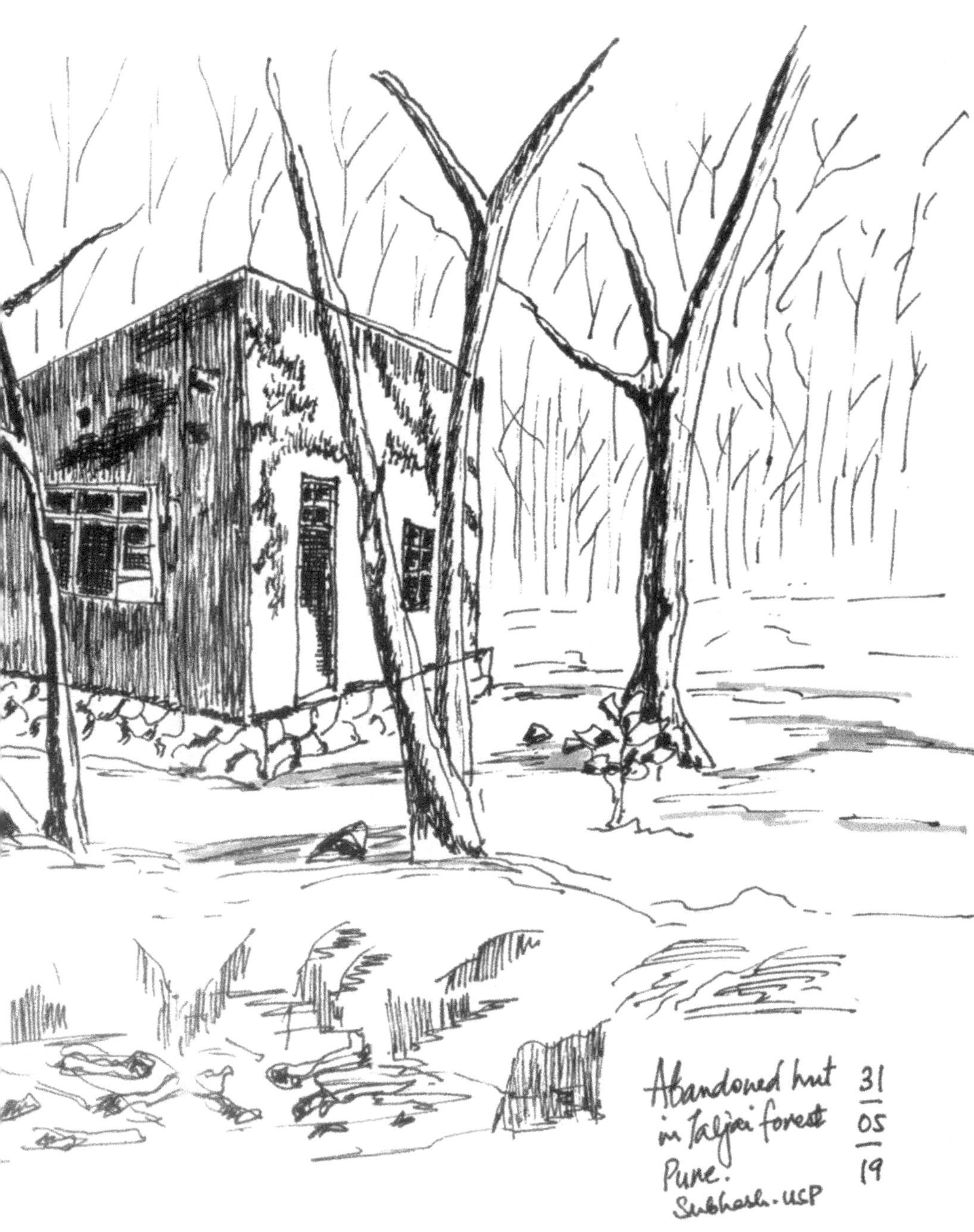

26

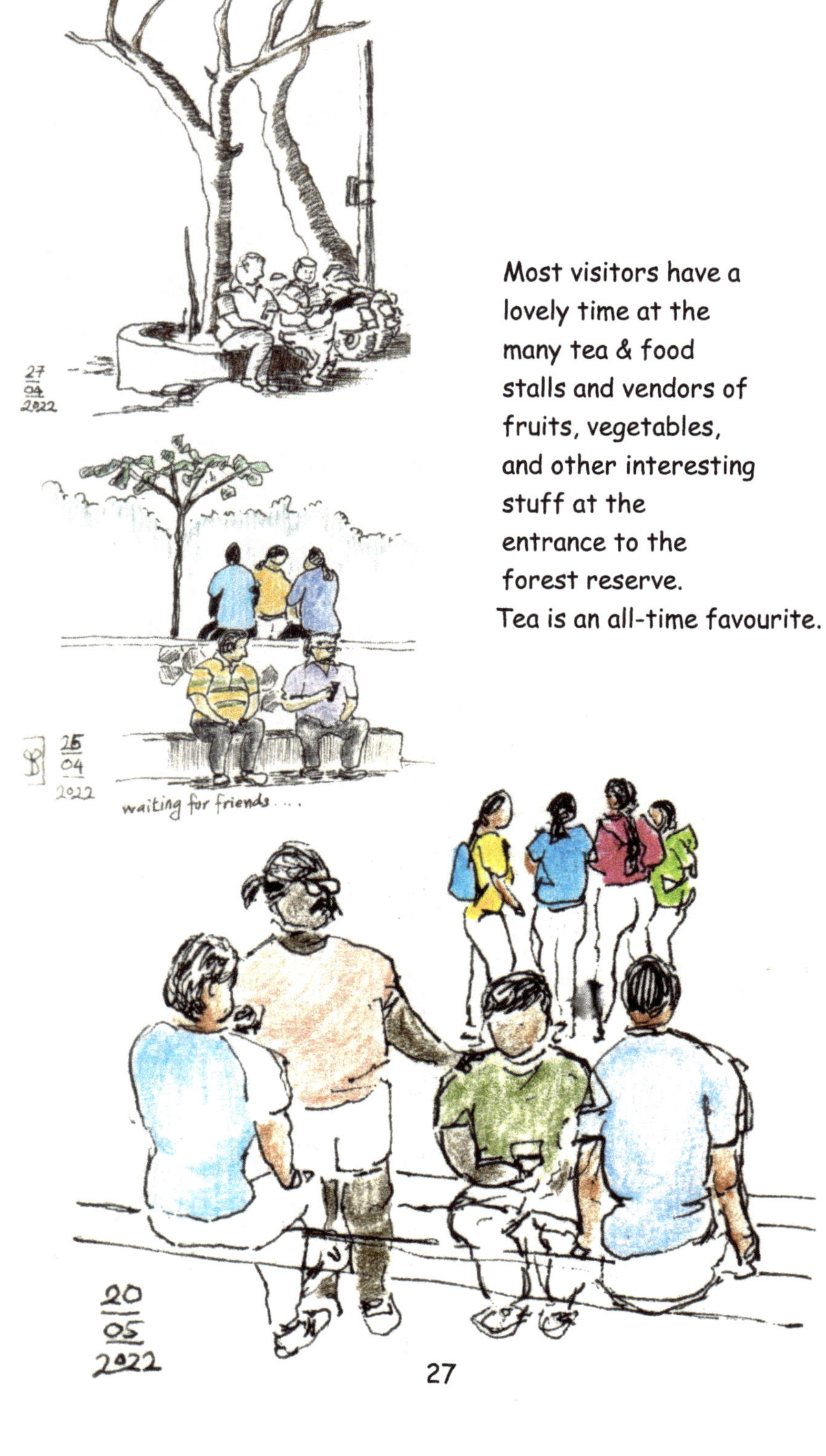

Most visitors have a
lovely time at the
many tea & food
stalls and vendors of
fruits, vegetables,
and other interesting
stuff at the
entrance to the
forest reserve.
Tea is an all-time favourite.

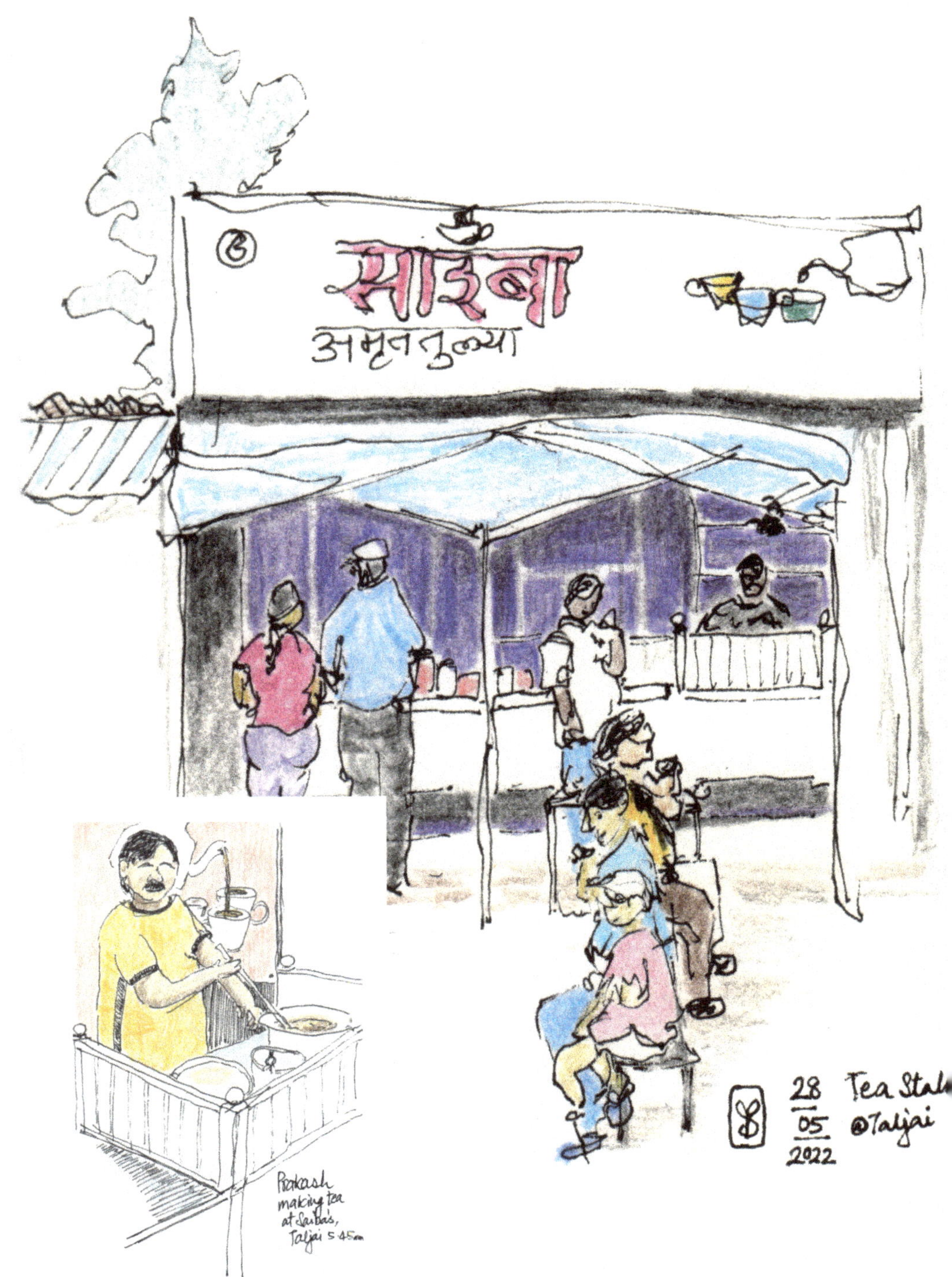

साईबा
अमृततुल्या
Prakash
making tea
at Saiba's,
Taljai 5.45am
28
05
2022
Tea Stall
@Taljai

And then there are the many vendors just outside the forest reserve gate, providing much needed sustenance after a good walk or workout. There is fresh fruits juice on offer as well as various supposedly healthy concoctions of various vegetables, smoothies, etc. Fresh coconut water beats the heat hands down.

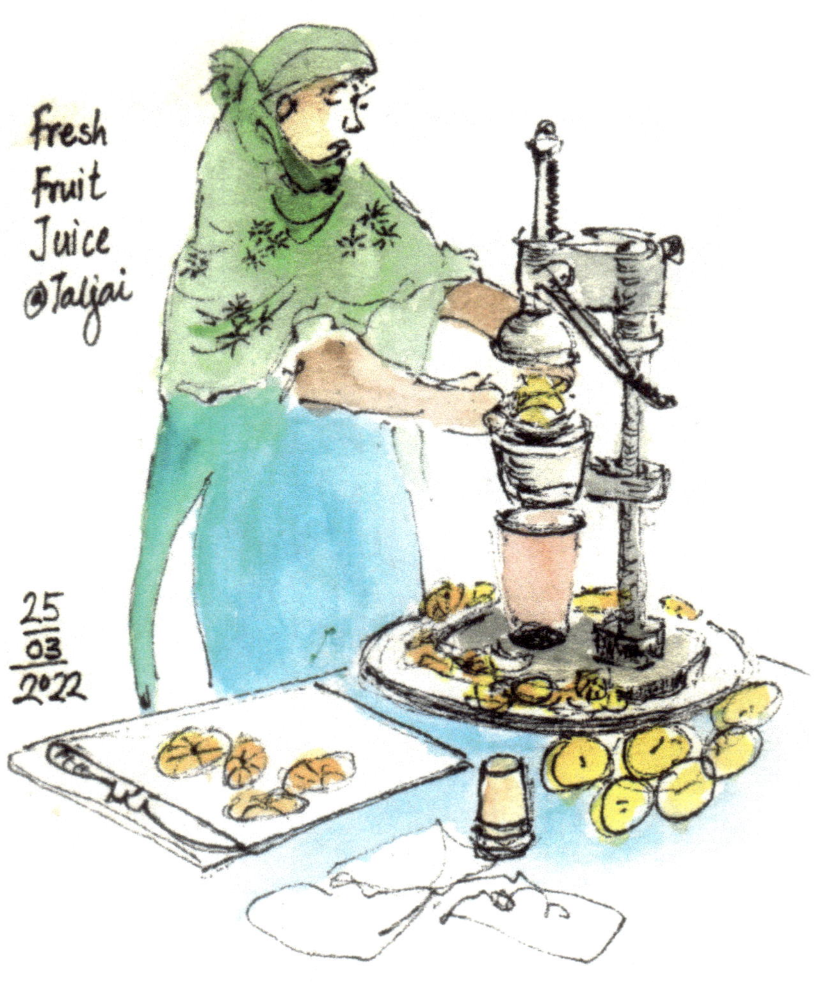

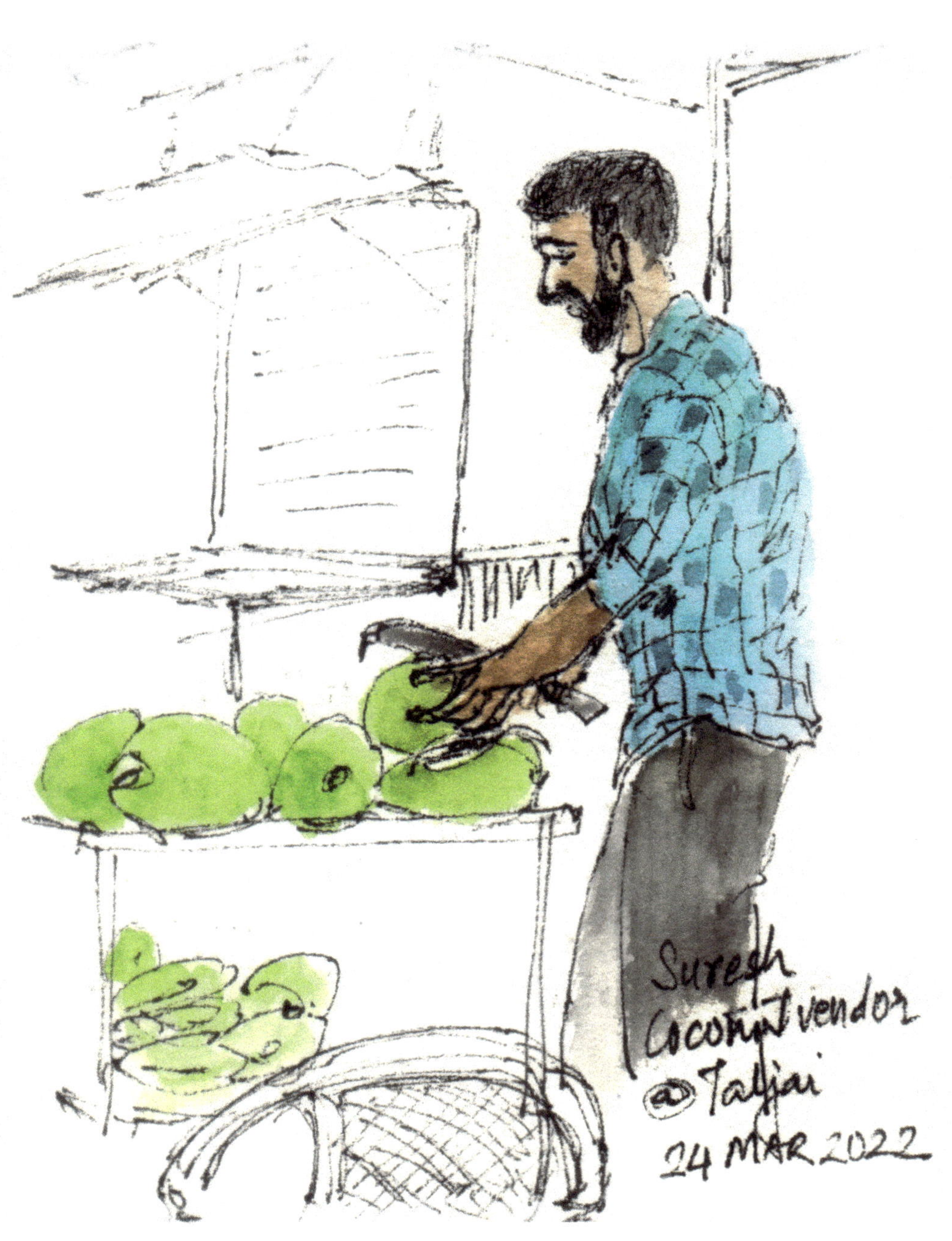

Suresh
Coconut vendor
@ Taljai
24 MAR 2022

As are the snacks. You need to top up all the calories that you burnt inside the forest. And so, there is a wide selection of snacks at hand, fried savories, all full of calories.

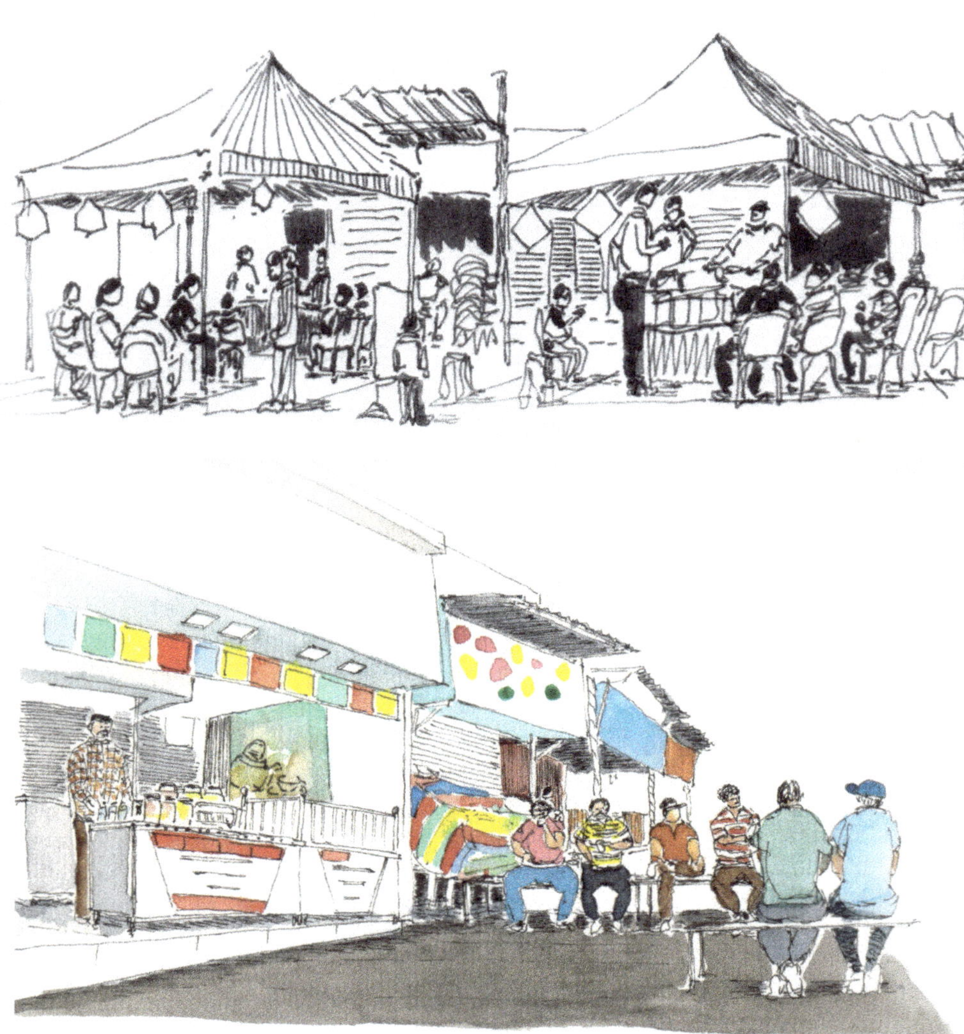

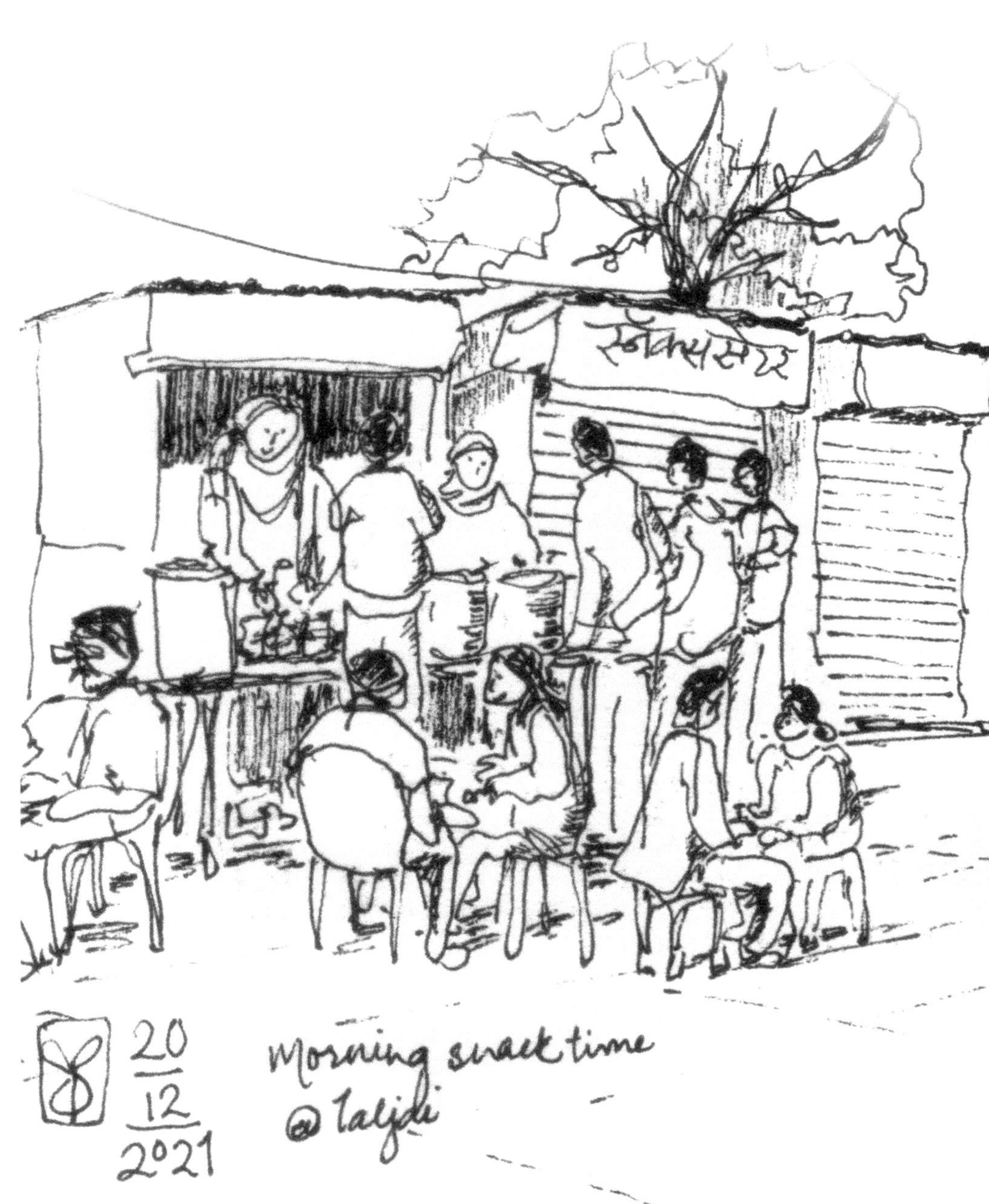
स्नेकस स्टर
20
12
2021
morning snack time
@ laljdi

People get their daily dose of veggies, fresh from the farm or the wholesale market, right at the door of the forest reserve. No need to go to a crowded market, where parking is always a problem.

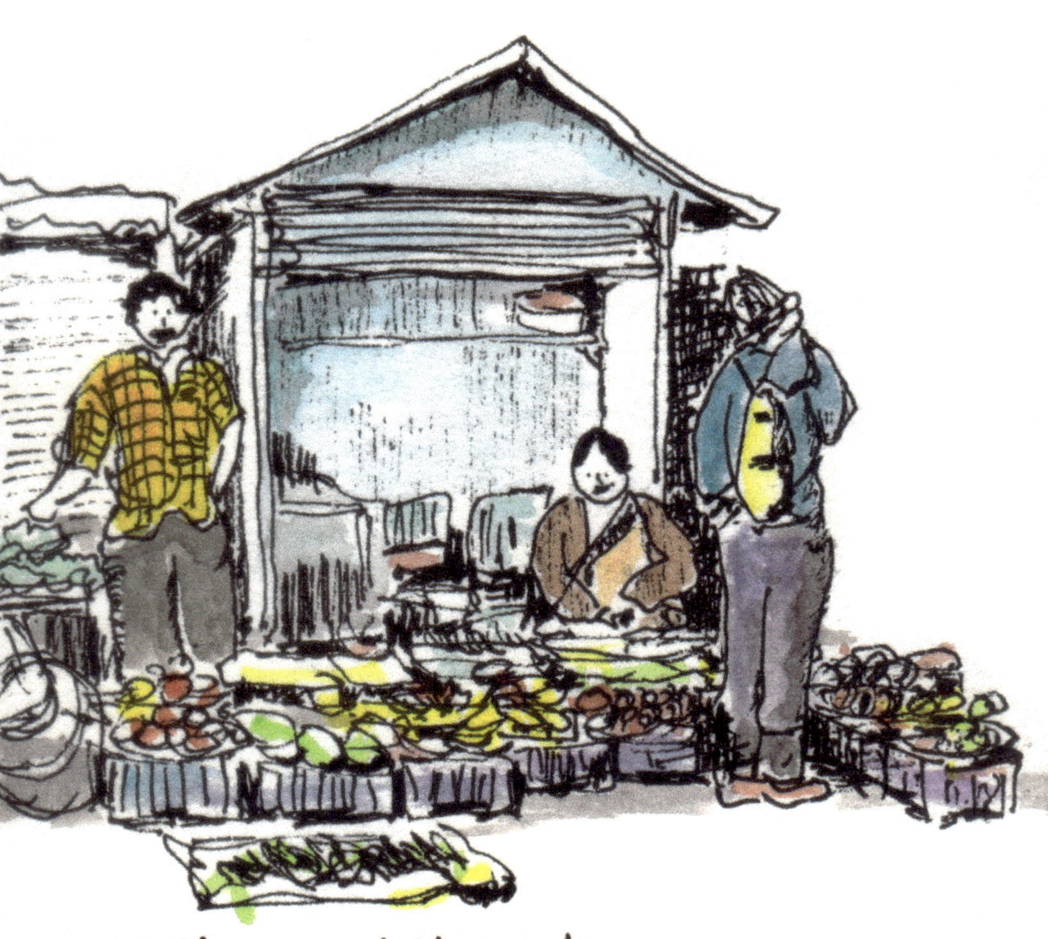

vegetable vendor
@ Taljai

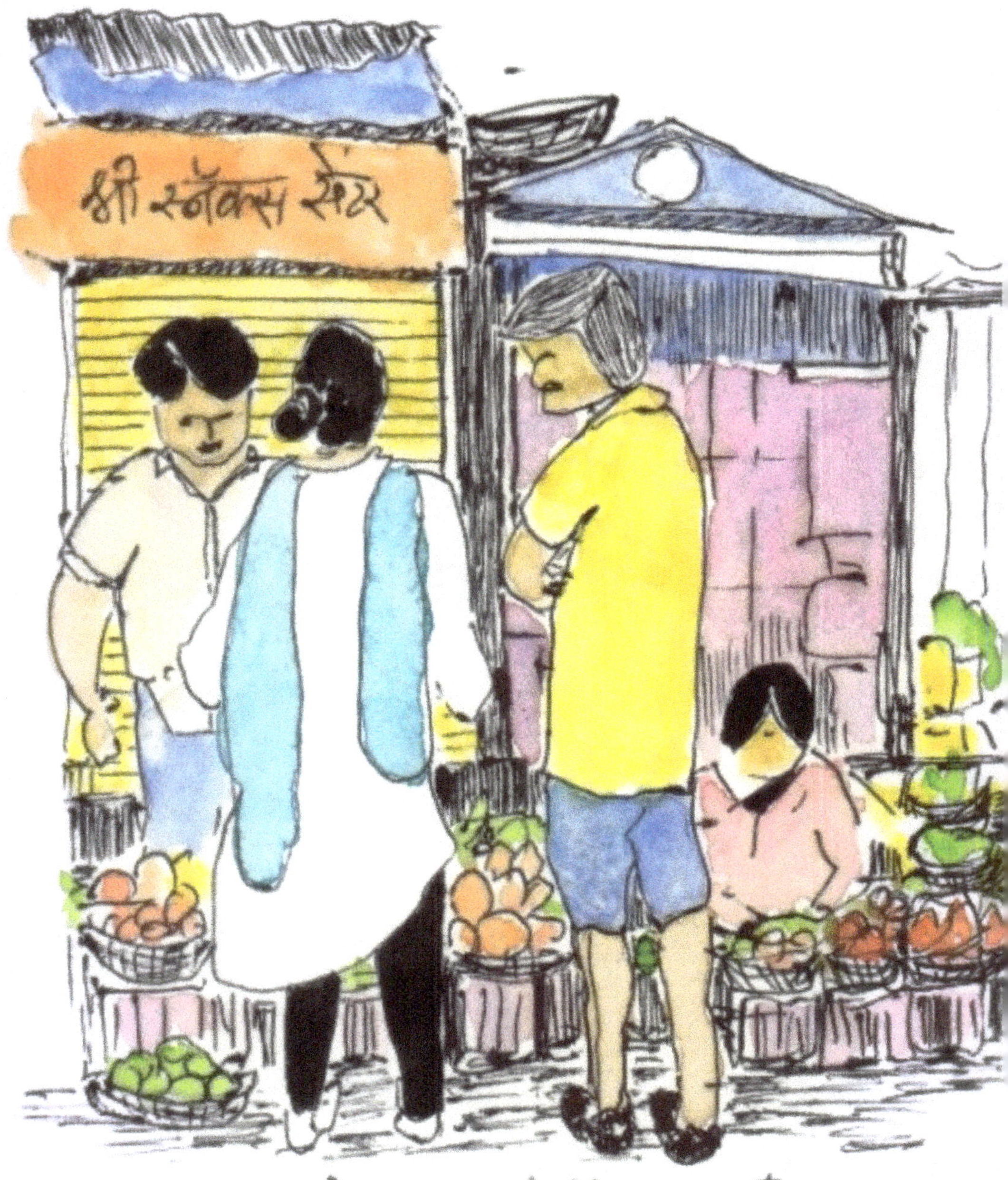

08
11
19
taijai fruit v vegetable market
morning walkers stocking up

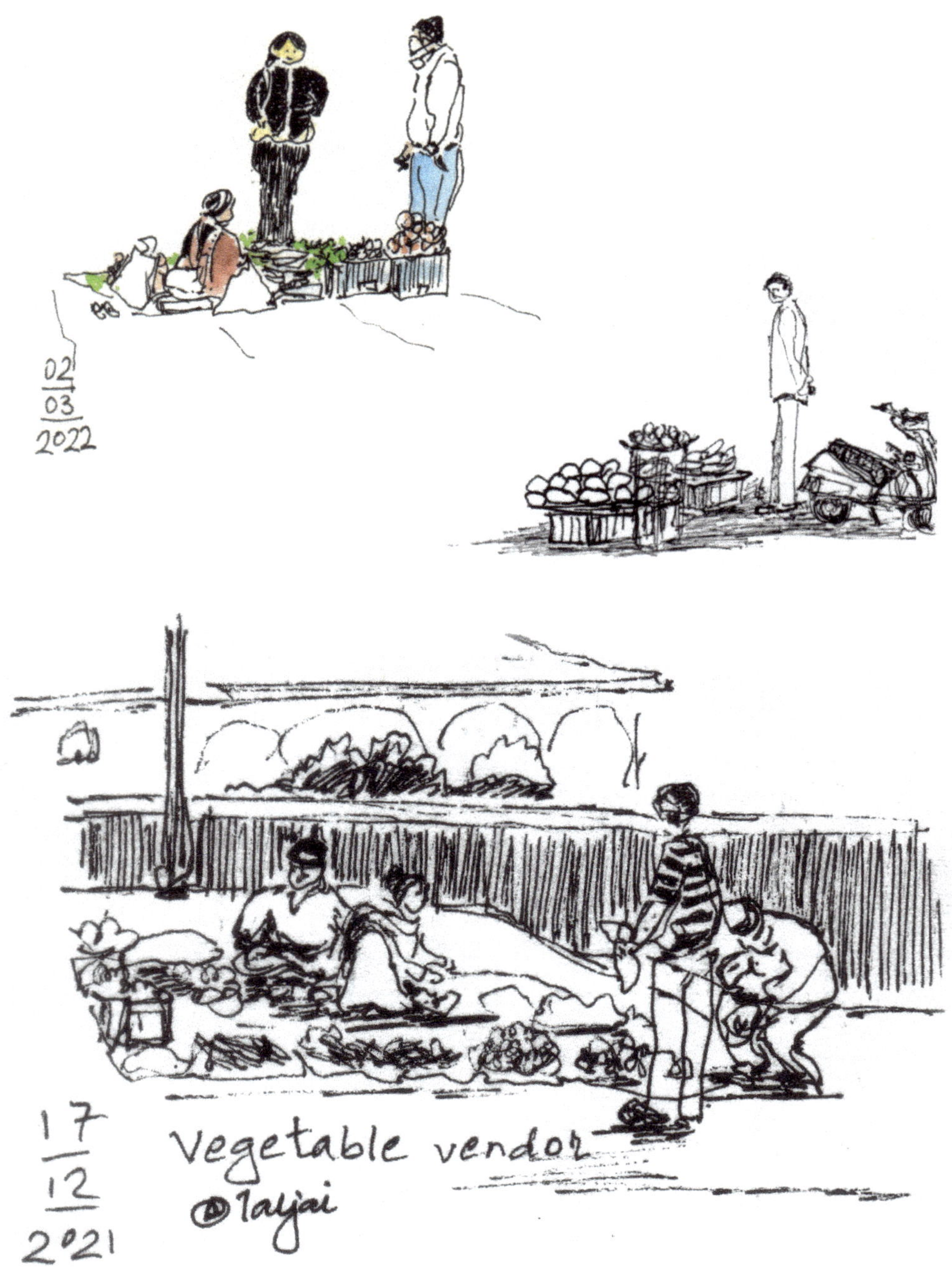

02
03
2022

17
12
2021

Vegetable vendor
@laijai

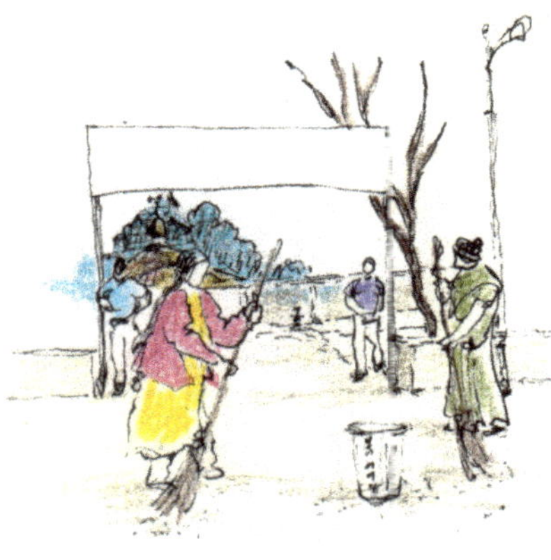

24/05/2022 Cleaning ladies @ work sweeping Taljai Temple

I started noticing and sketching unimportant things and glimpses of life happening around me. The early morning street sweepers and cleaners making the place ready for the crowds, tradespeople setting up their stalls, etc.

There was this young boy feeding some pups regularly. He must be driving his mom crazy, with all the food he brings from home. It was great to see such a young boy show so much commitment, to do this every day.

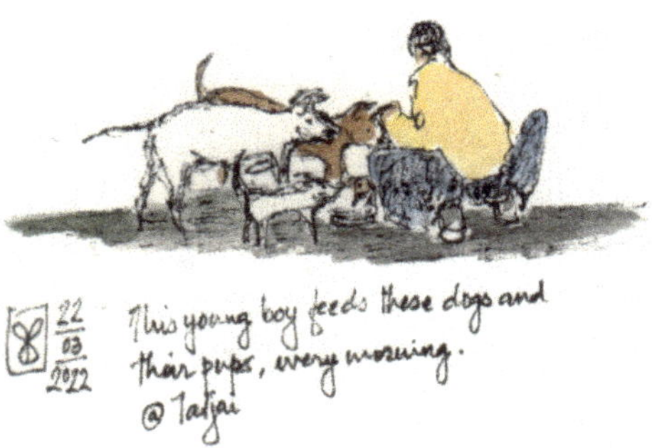

22/03/2022 This young boy feeds these dogs and their pups, every morning. @ Taljai

The small vendors
plying their trade

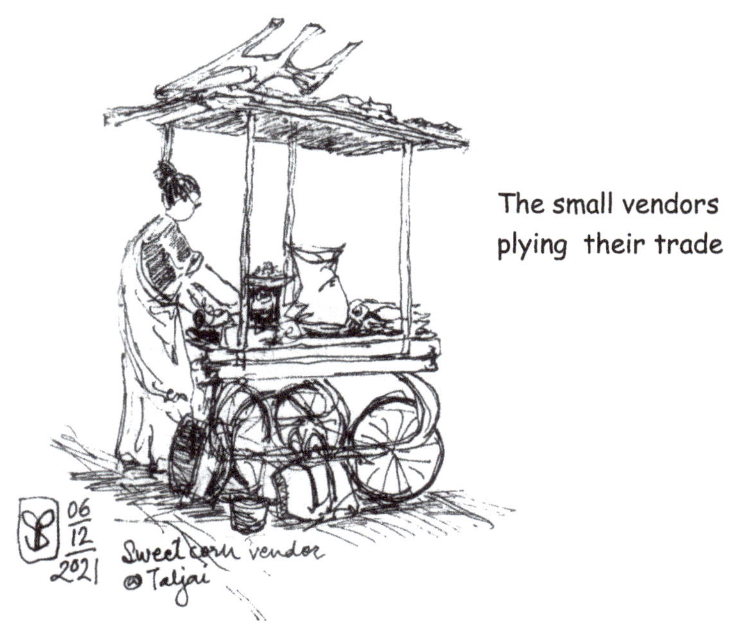

The view of part of the city from the top of the hill

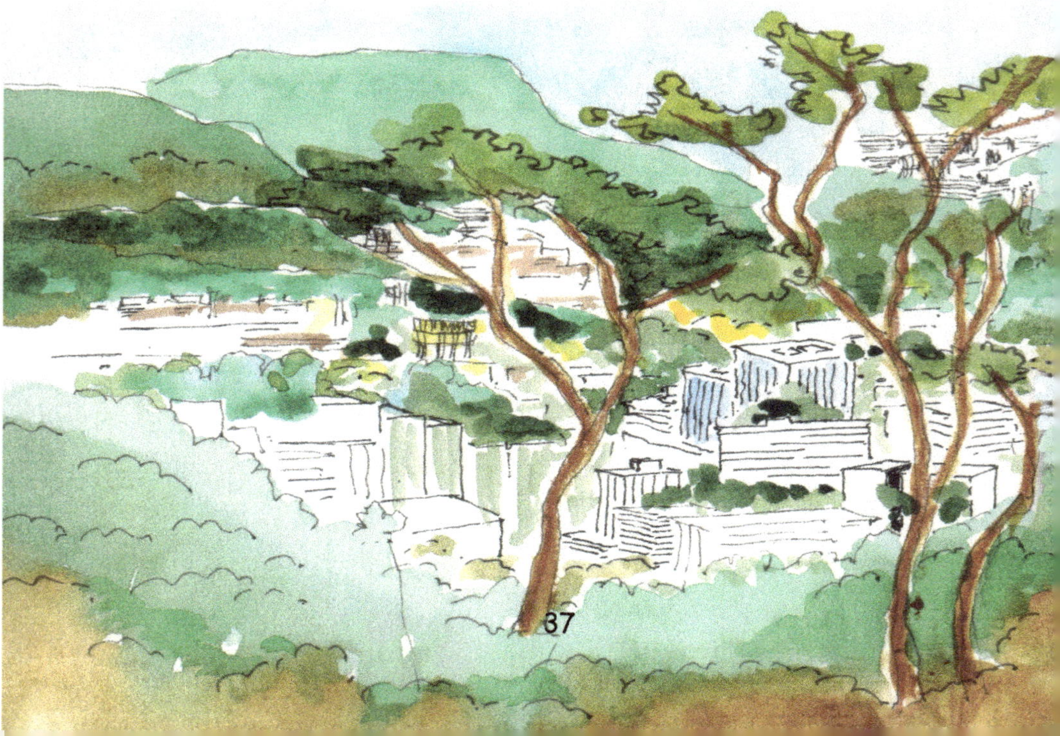

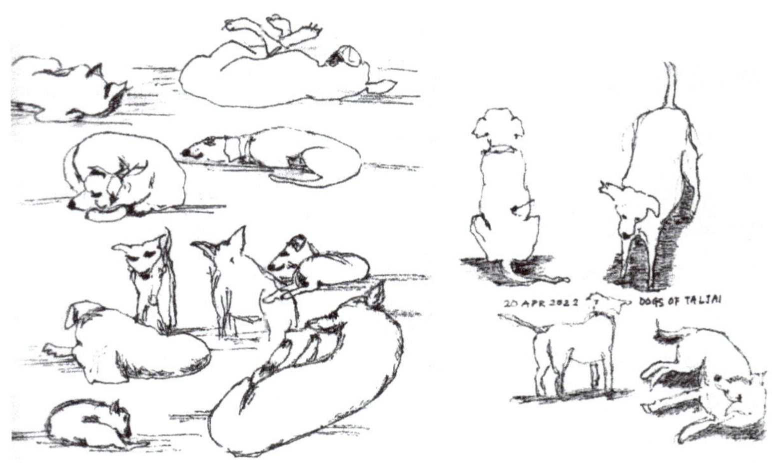

The dogs at Taljai generally have an enjoyable time and provide excellent pet therapy for the visitors.

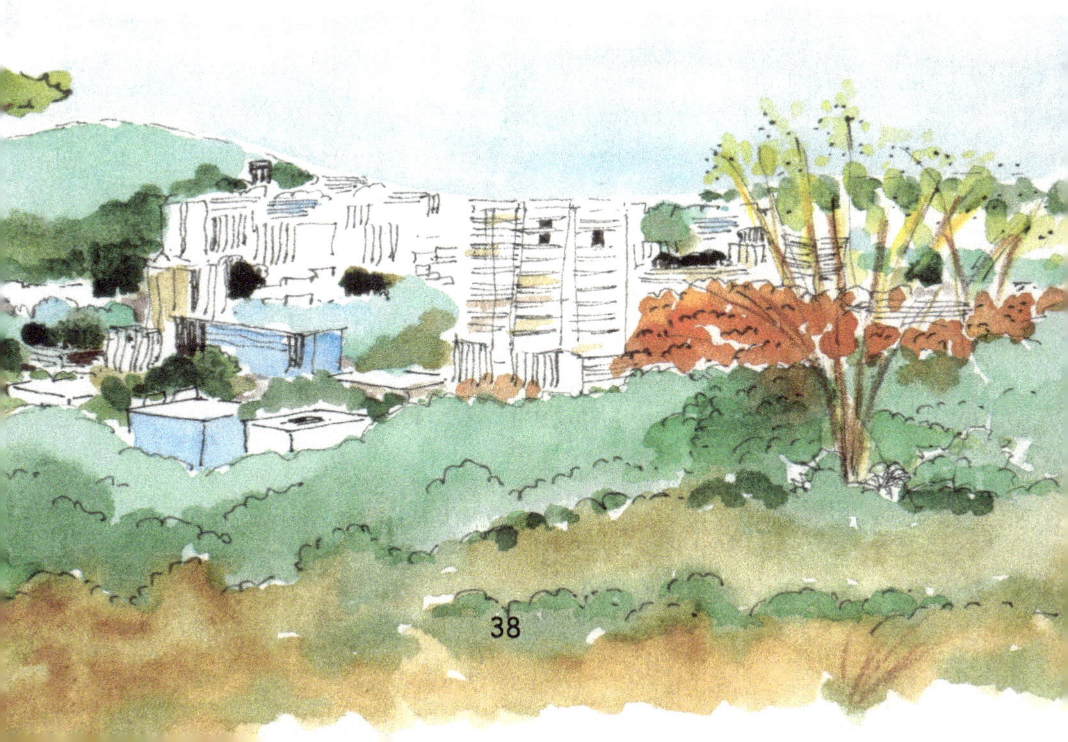

I have tried sketching on the go while walking in the forest.
While the results are a bit shaky, they capture the essence
of the scene.

There are lovely spots within the forest, providing water for the birds and animals. Many people bring grains for the peacocks.

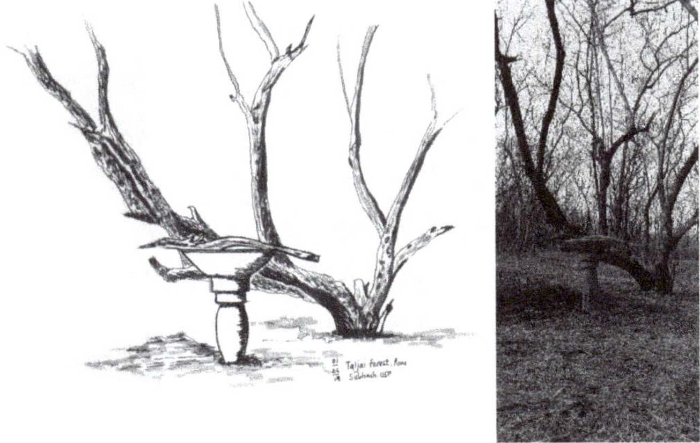

This lovely spot no longer exists, as it was levelled out and replanted recently. So, this is the only memory that I or the readers can have and share, of this beautifully shaped cistern full of water, under the boughs of a spreading tree, seen stark and leafless in its dry summer avatar.

There are many such places and things now disappearing or changing, which my friends and I have been sketching and documenting, which speak of the days gone by and the places that were. Documenting a part of history, as it were.

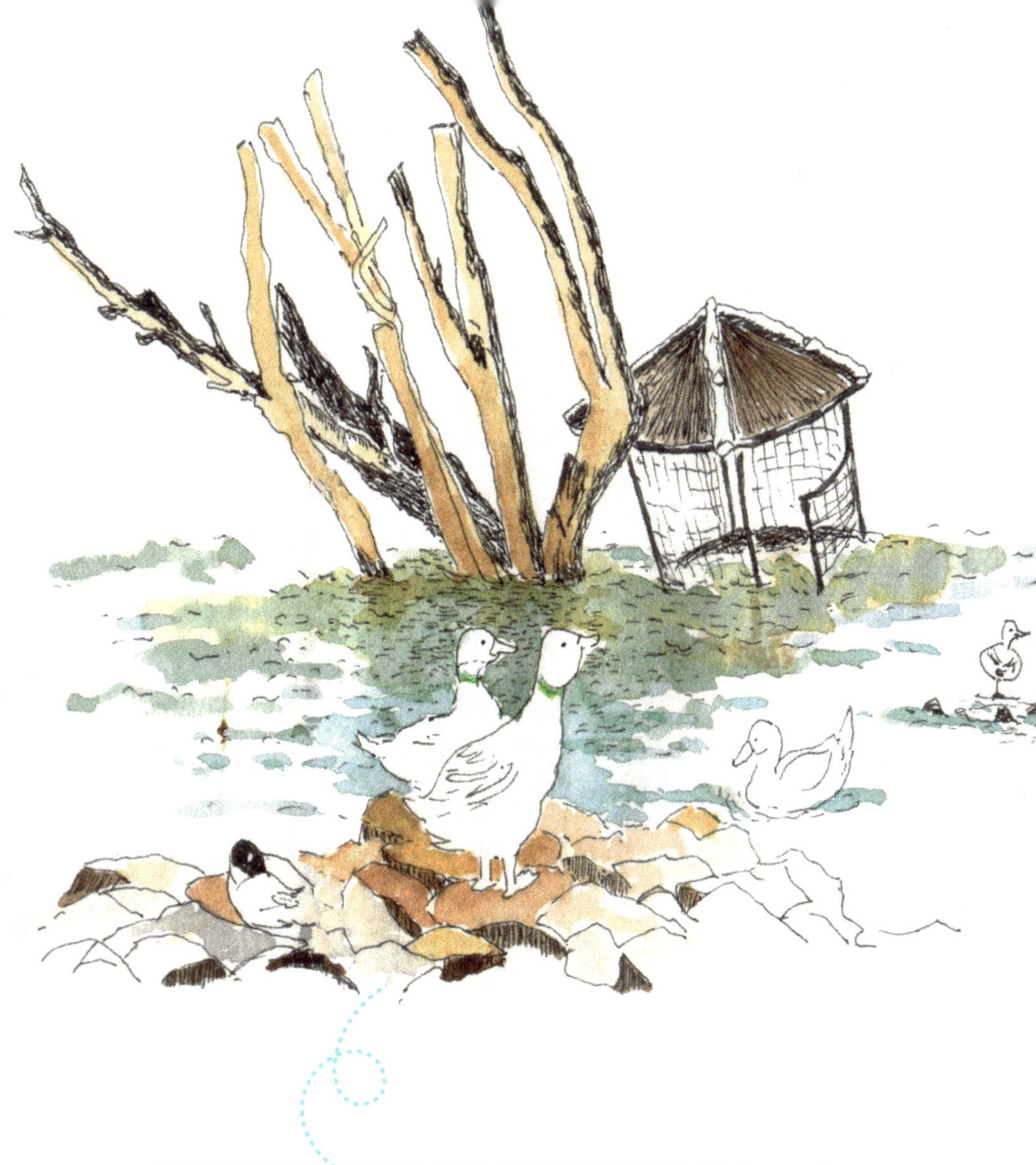

There are several waterbodies within the forest for ducks and other birds and animals.

Initially, I started sketching people having tea, buying vegetables or like me, waiting for their friends.

Since I carried a small sketchbook in my pocket, I could also sketch inside the forest, whenever we stopped for a breather or for a long look at the lovely forest vistas, drinking in

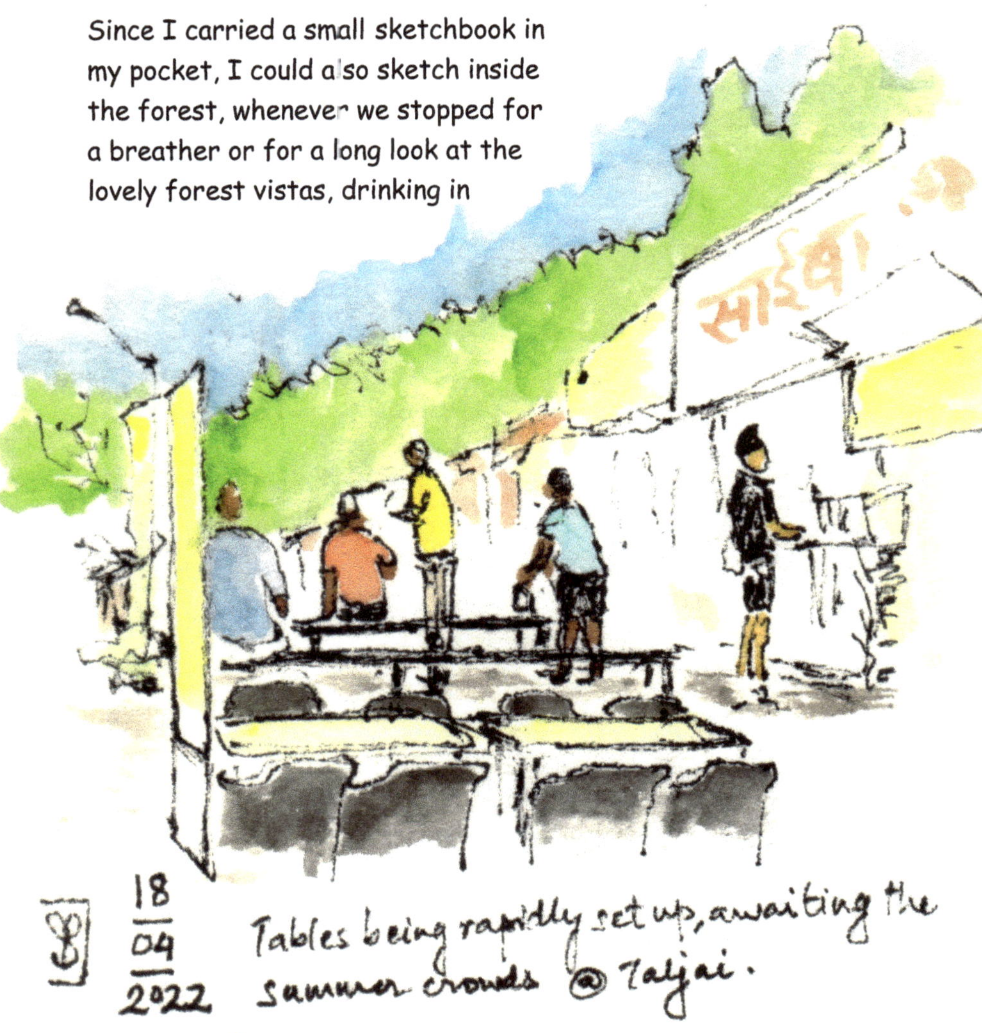

18
04
2022

Tables being rapidly set up, awaiting the summer crowds @ Taljai.

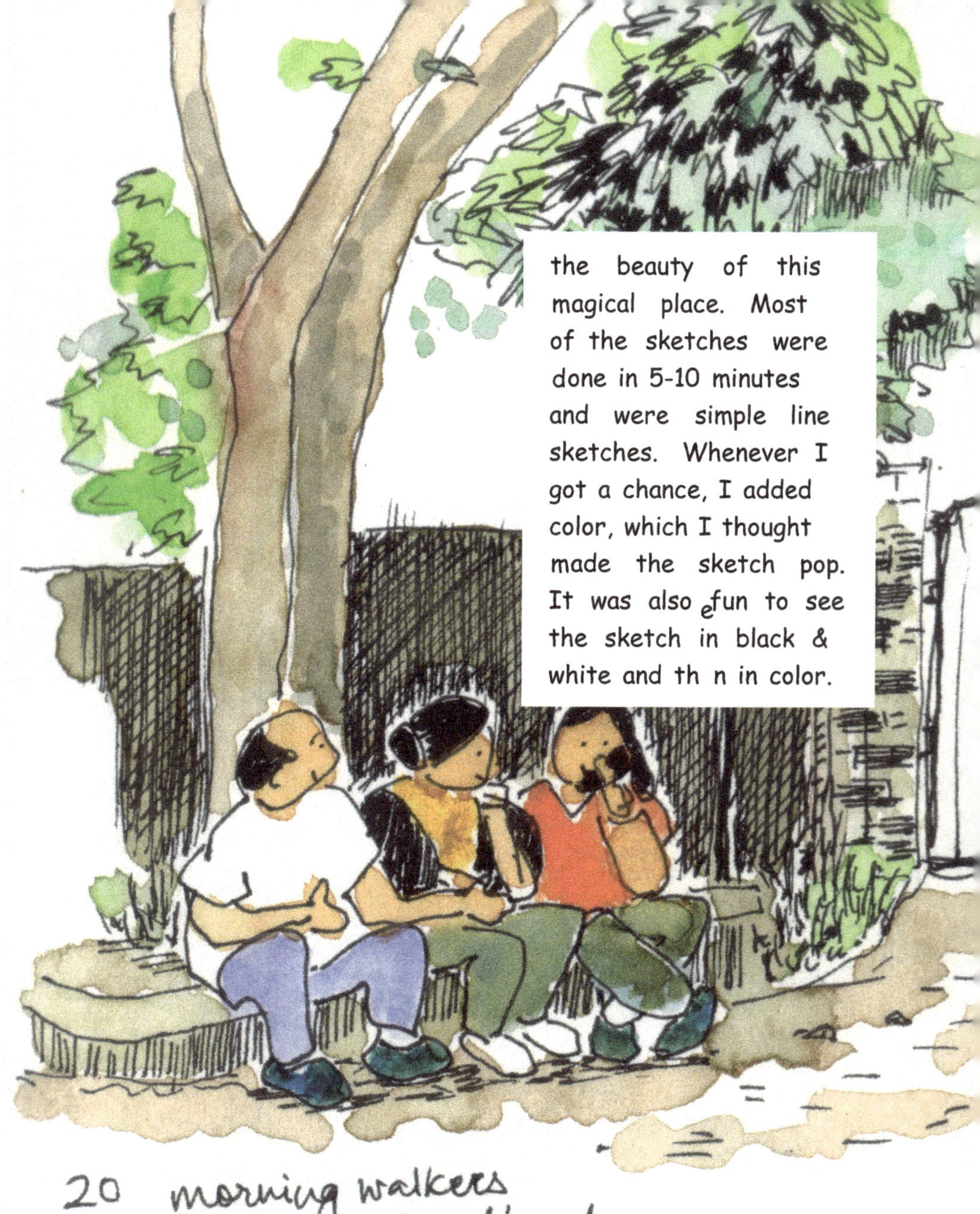

the beauty of this magical place. Most of the sketches were done in 5-10 minutes and were simple line sketches. Whenever I got a chance, I added color, which I thought made the sketch pop. It was also fun to see the sketch in black & white and th n in color.

20
11
19
morning walkers
taking a relaxed break
at the Jaljai Forest Gate
subhash.usp

Sketching people is interesting. It allows for a quick capture of people going about their tasks, enjoying themselves or exerting at the workouts. Soon people started noticing that I was sketching, and they would sometimes come over to see what I was doing. Many liked to see the process and asked questions. They soon became part of my large group of Taljai friends and followers on Instagram.

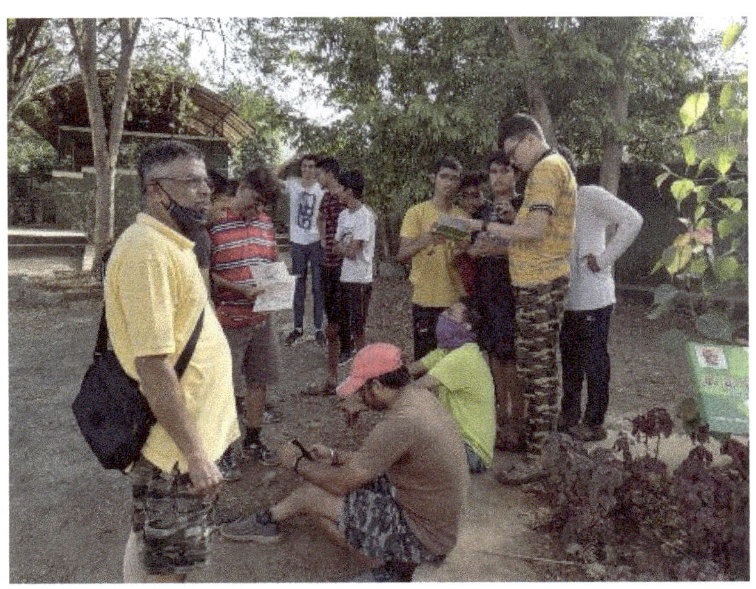

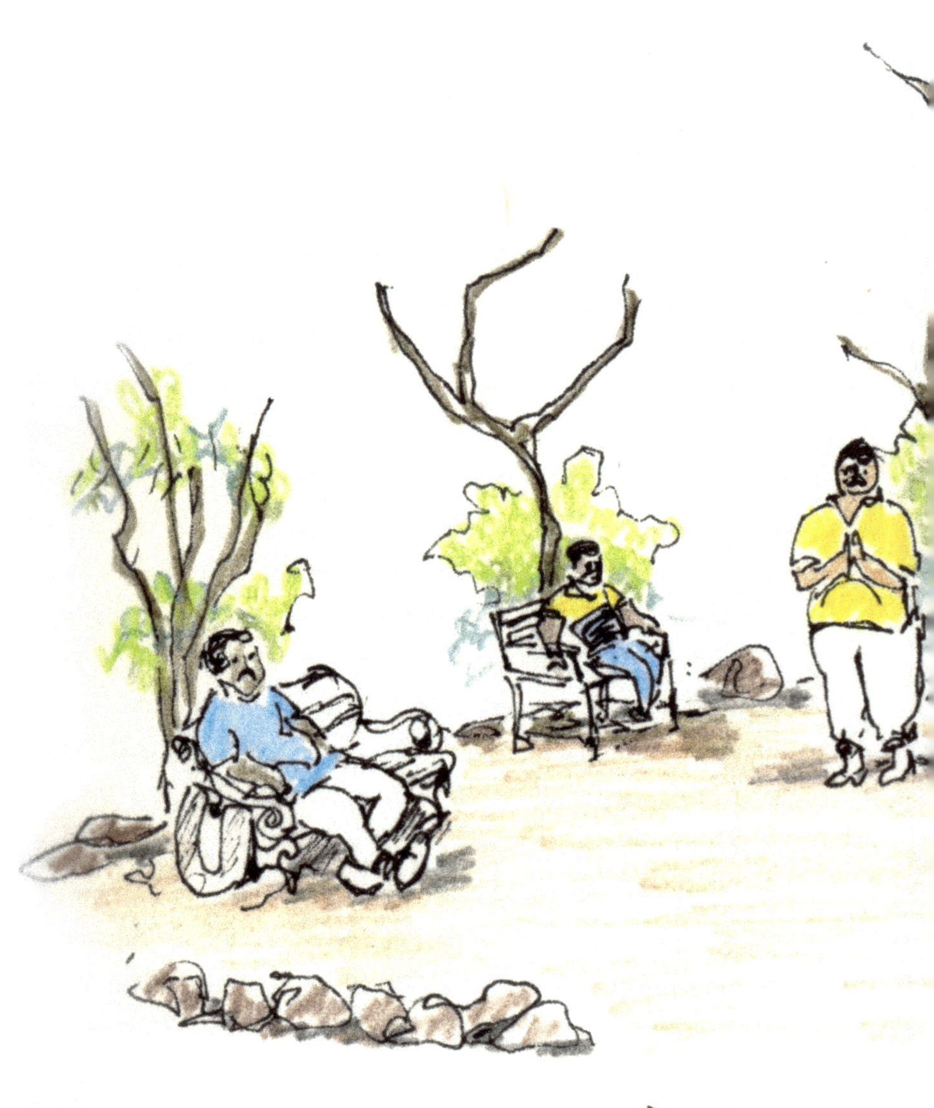

31
05
2022

Exercise group in the forest @Taljai

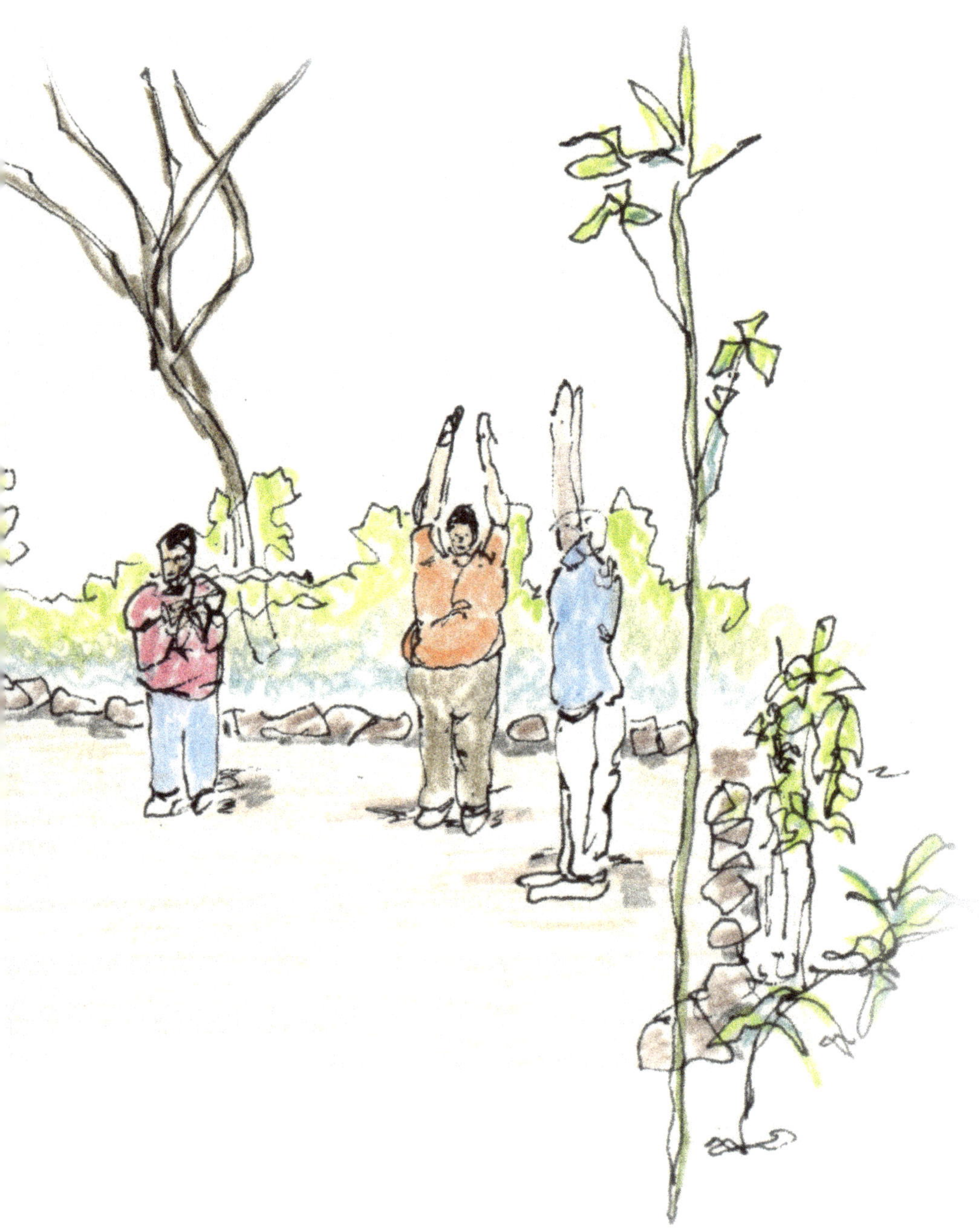

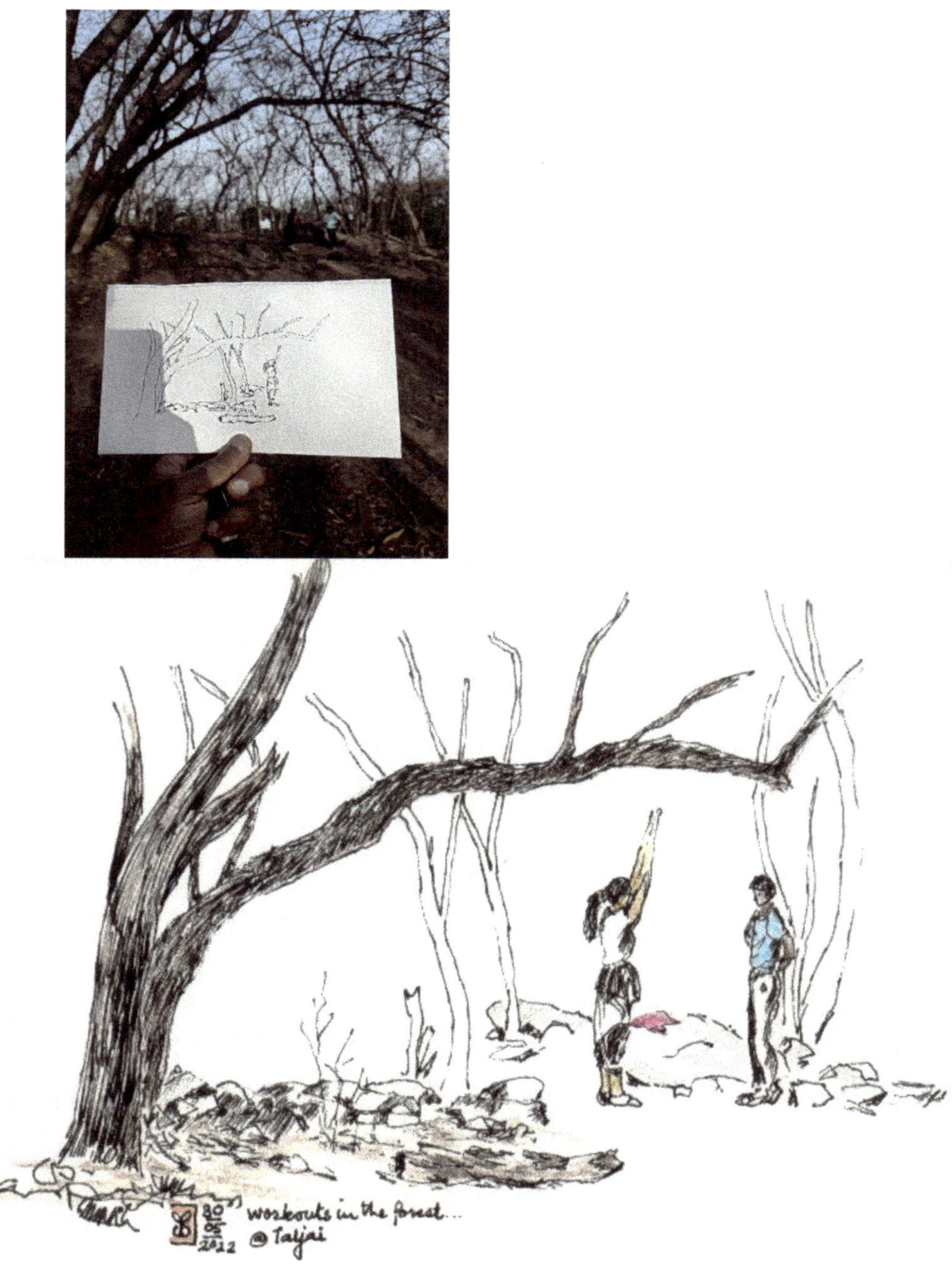
workouts in the forest...
@ Taijai

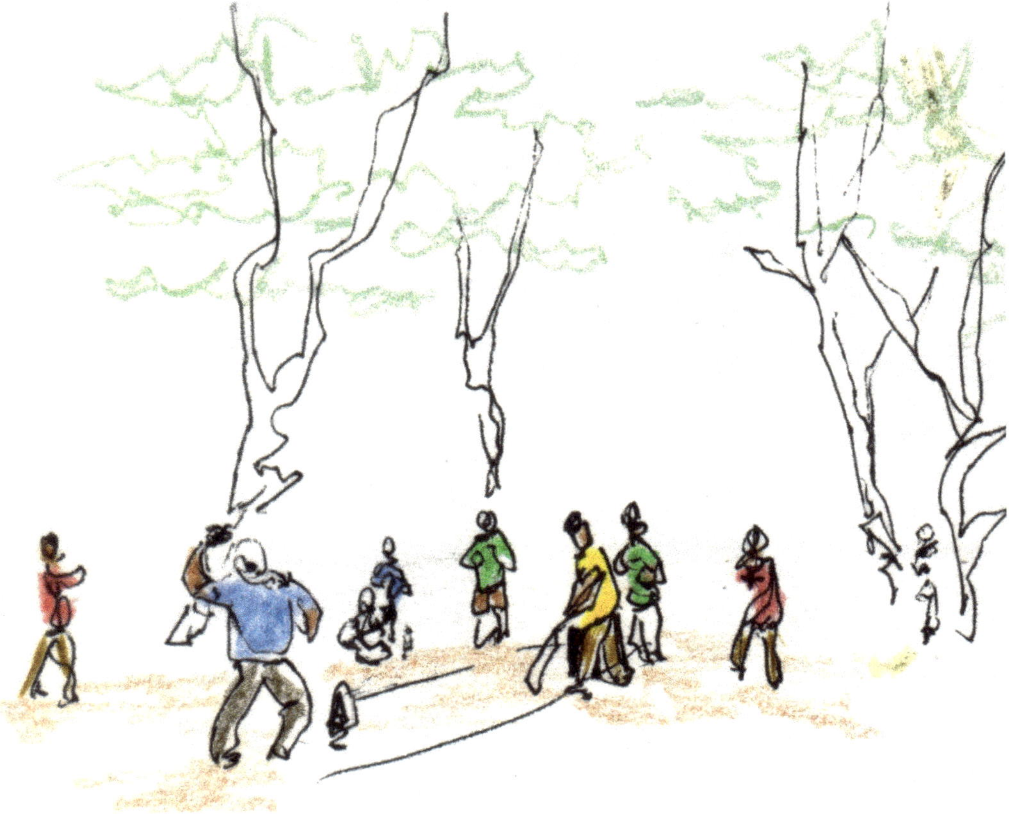

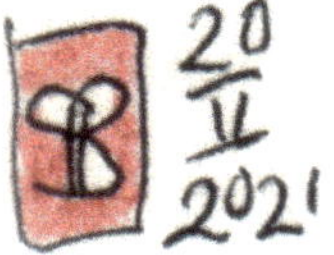

Cricket is a religion in India. During cricket season, youngsters will find a way to play the game even in the middle of the forest.

Yoga is very popular in India and the forest is a great place to practice it, either individually or together in a group. I sketched this young woman who was sitting high up on the slope, amongst the trees and was lit up by the rising sun, which was almost parallel to her.

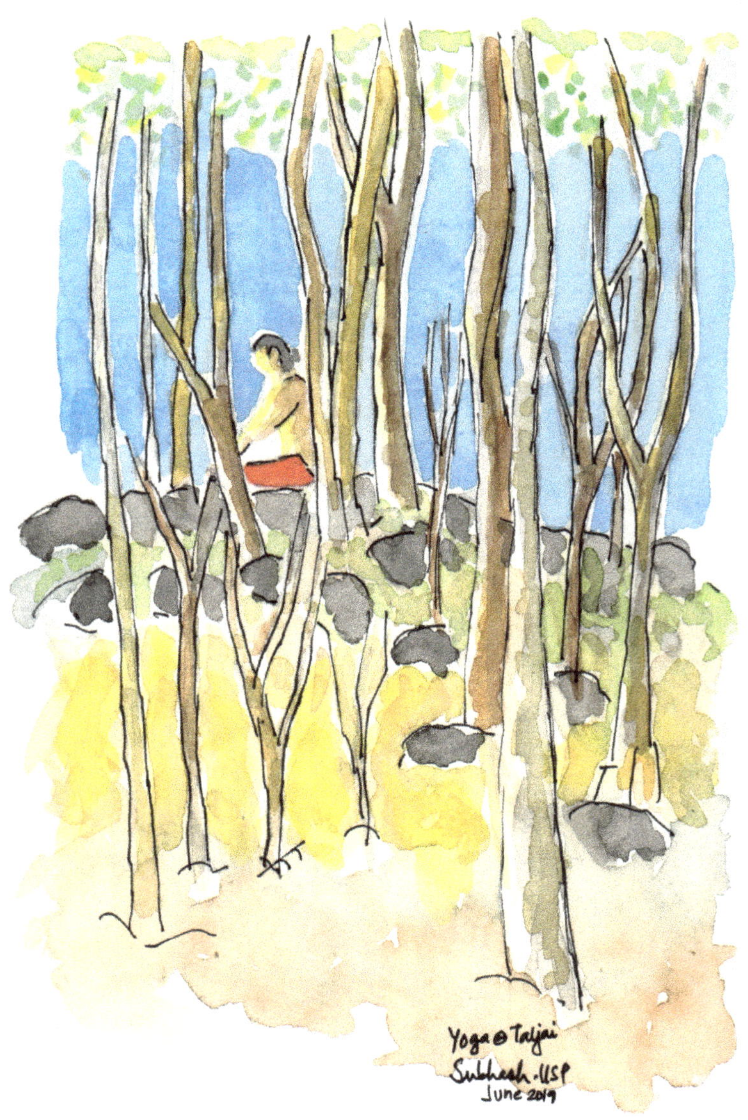

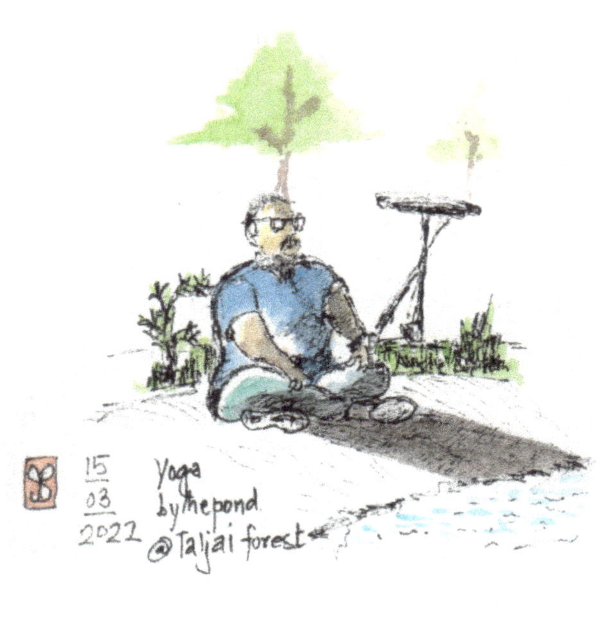

15
03
2022
Yoga
by the pond
@ Taljai forest

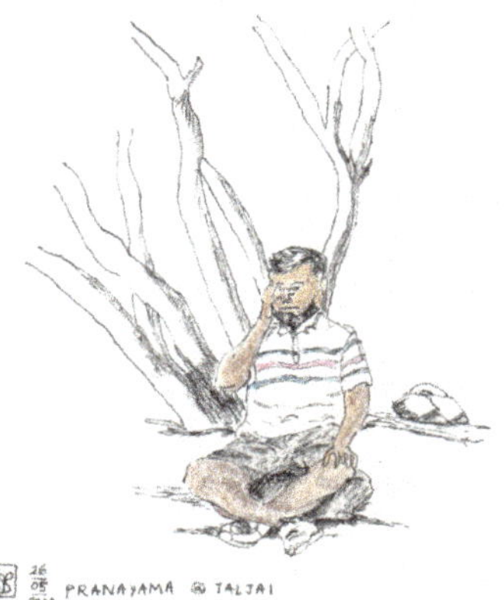

26
05
2022
PRANAYAMA @ TALJAI

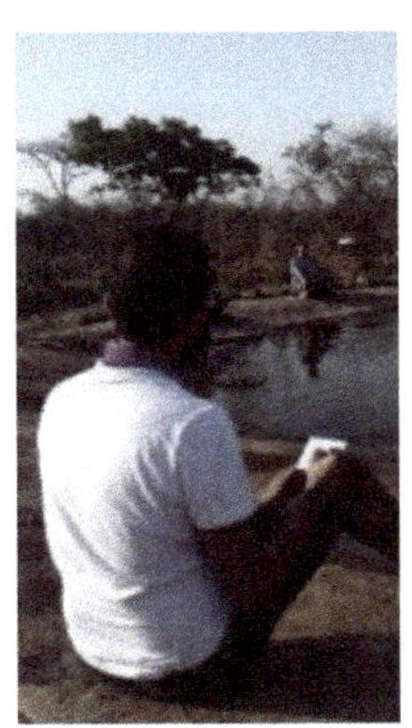

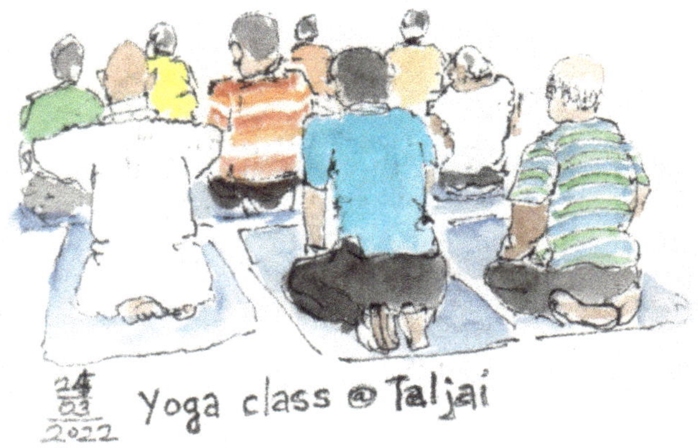

24
03
2022
Yoga class @ Taljai

The many moods of the forest

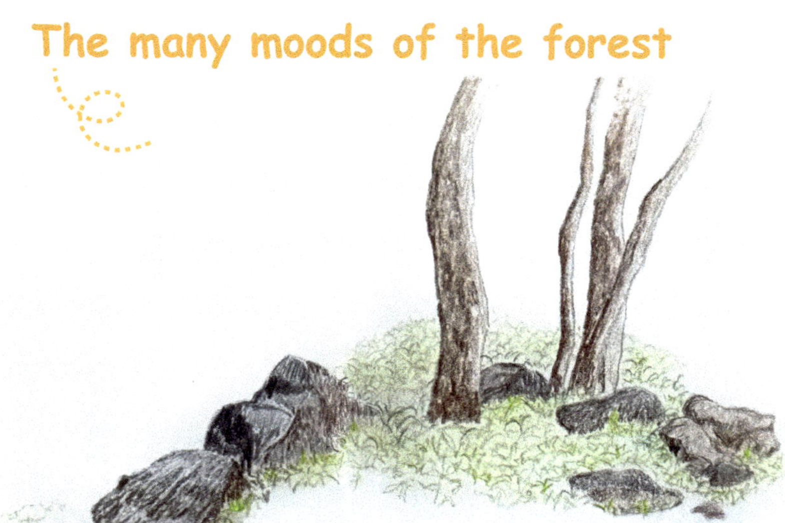

The Taljai forest provides ever-changing vistas through the seasons.

Summers are quite hot and dry in Pune and many of the trees lose all their foliage and bear a stark bare look during the scorching summer months.

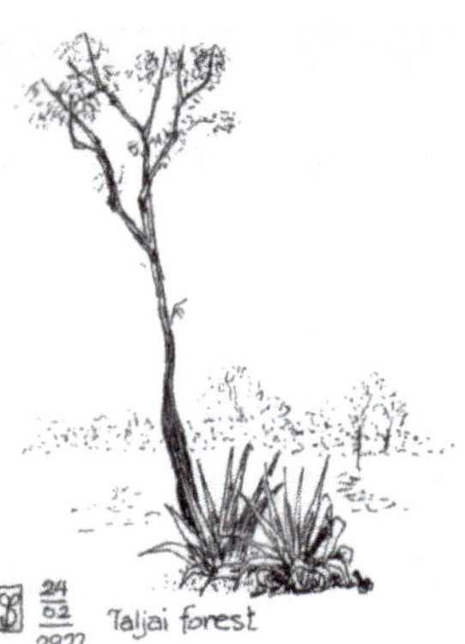

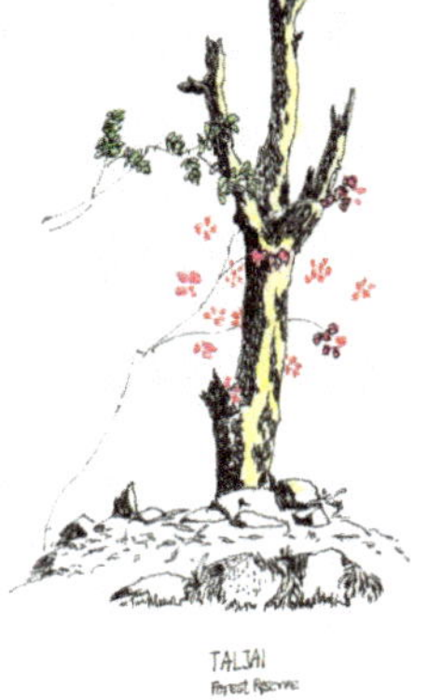

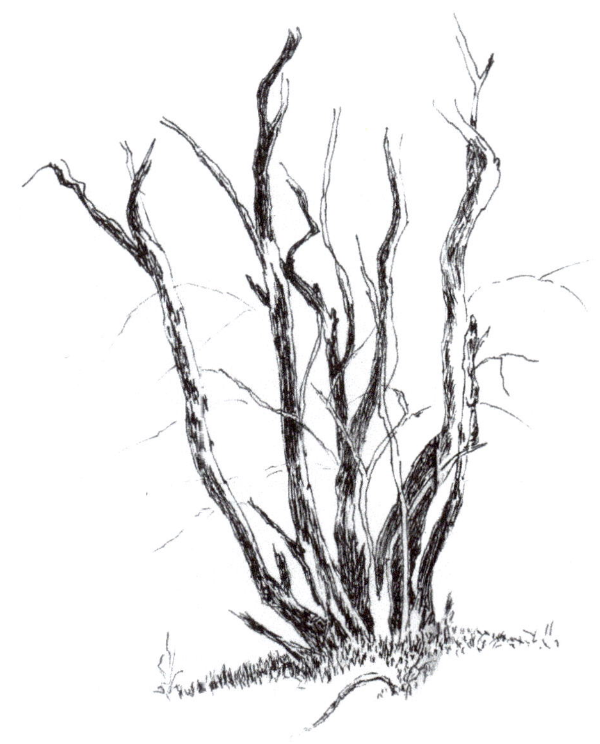

This changes dramatically during the monsoons when the forest turns lush and verdant with a hundred shades of green.

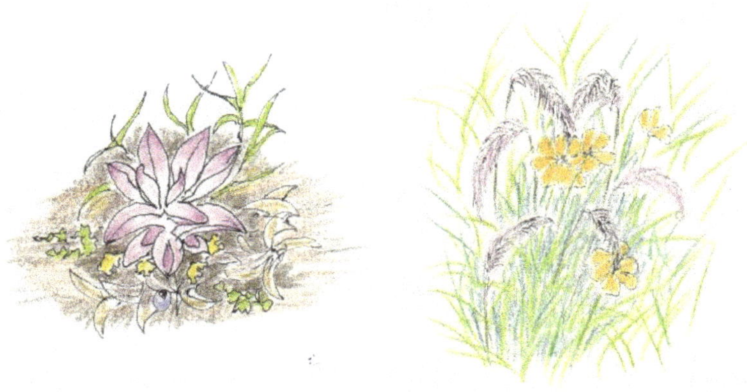

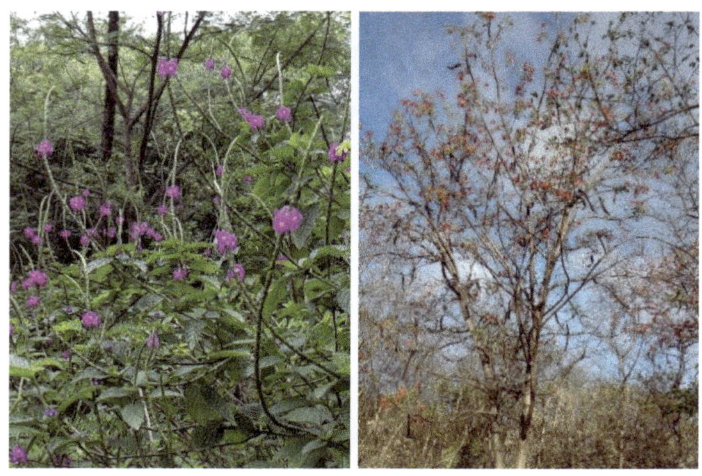

Winter brings mist and obscures the view of the trees and the landscape, adding mystery to the walks.

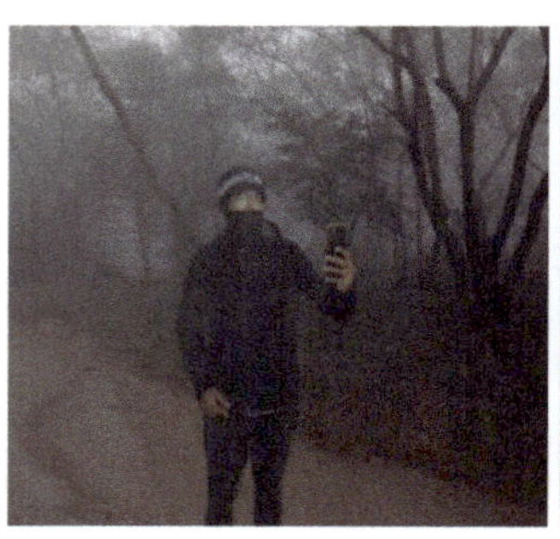
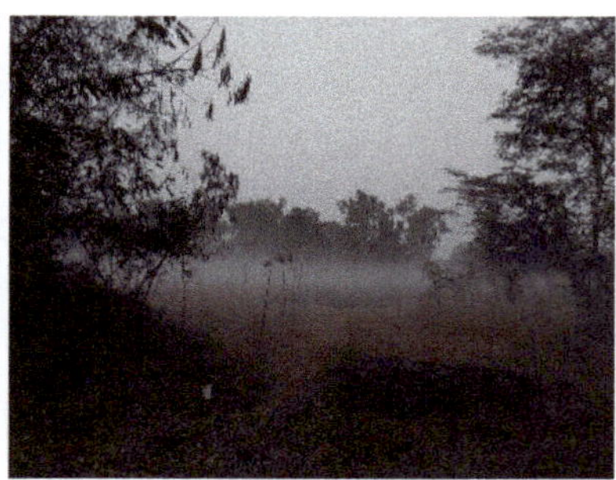

Taljai Mata Mandir

The Taljai Mata Temple, by which this area is recognised, is just outside the forest gate.

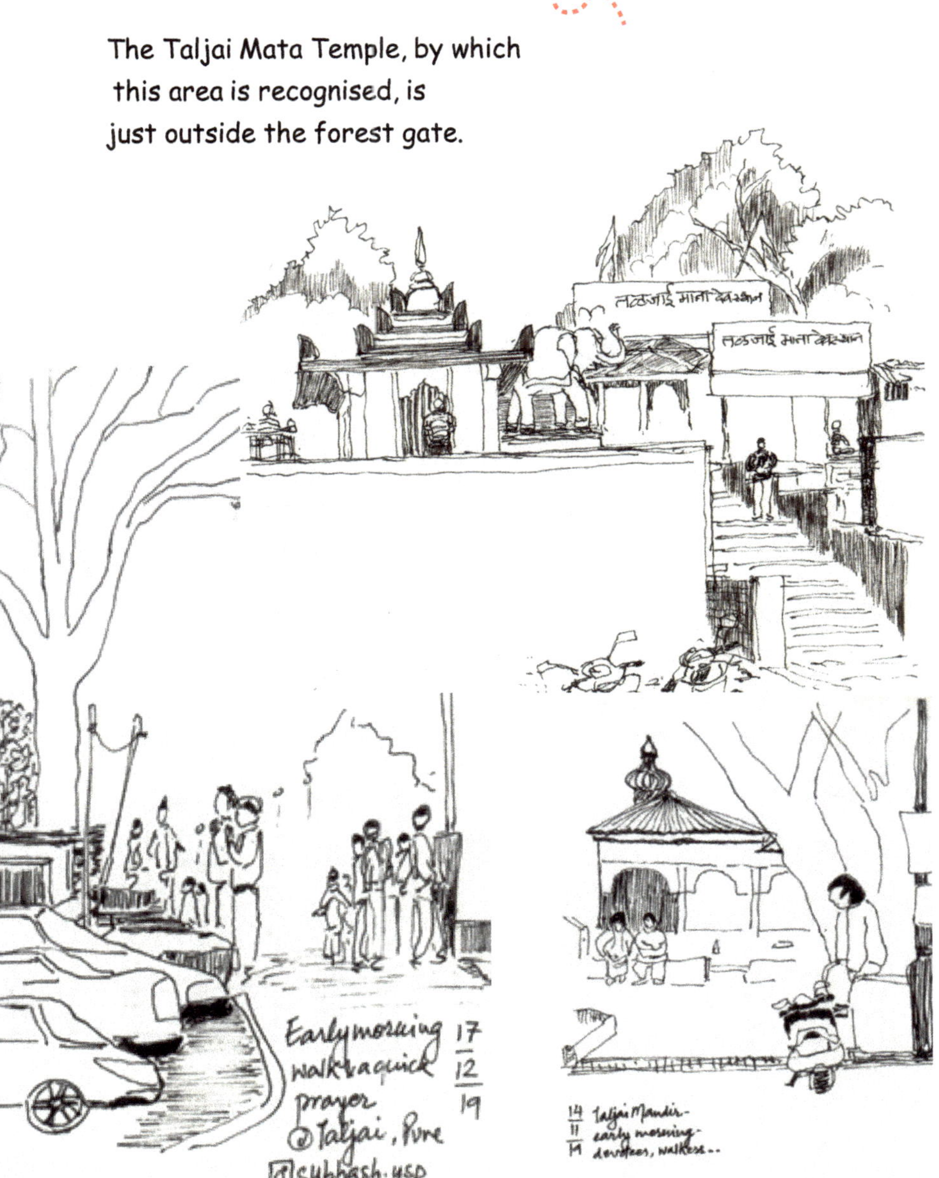

The Navratri festival and Dussera, which celebrate the fight and victory of Goddess Durga over the demon Mahishasura, usually draw heavy crowds for the 9 days of the festival. Ladies from all over the city, come fully decked up in their finery, to pray to and ask for blessings from the Taljai Mata Devi (goddess). Stalls are set up to cater to the needs of the pilgrims, for puja material, snacks, etc. and they do brisk business during these 10 days.

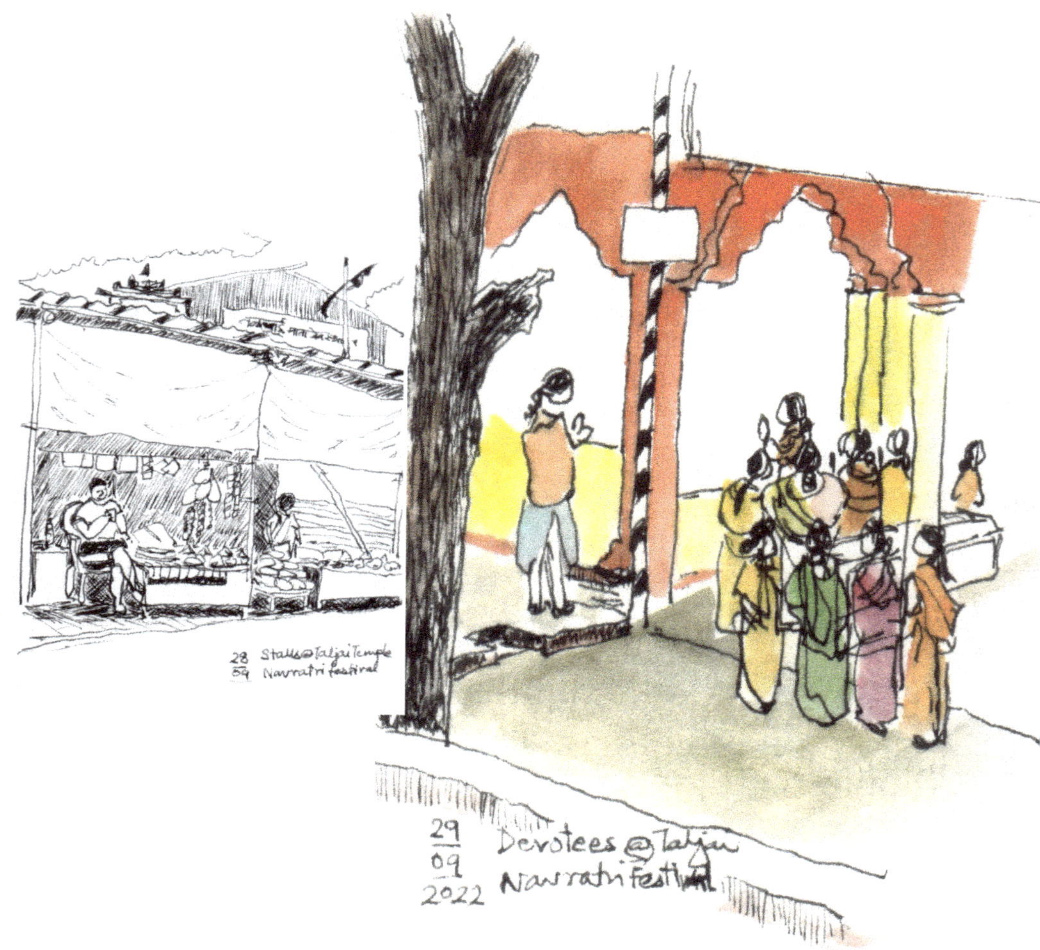

The annual Pandharpur Waari pilgrimmage which holds the distinction of being the oldest, spontaneous and unbroken tradition spanning over 3 centuries, halts in Pune. The pilgrims are spread out all over the city and some make a halt at the Taljai temple for a few days. A truck usually carries their small packs of luggage and a mobile kitchen, with them for about 45 days. I have walked with them for part of the way and found their spirit and energy divinely inspired. There are no organisers for the hundreds of thousand people who walk this pilgrimmage spanning about 45 days, yet there are no problems that cannot be solved amicably by and within themselves. The discipline and humility of these ordinary farmfolk is simply amazing.

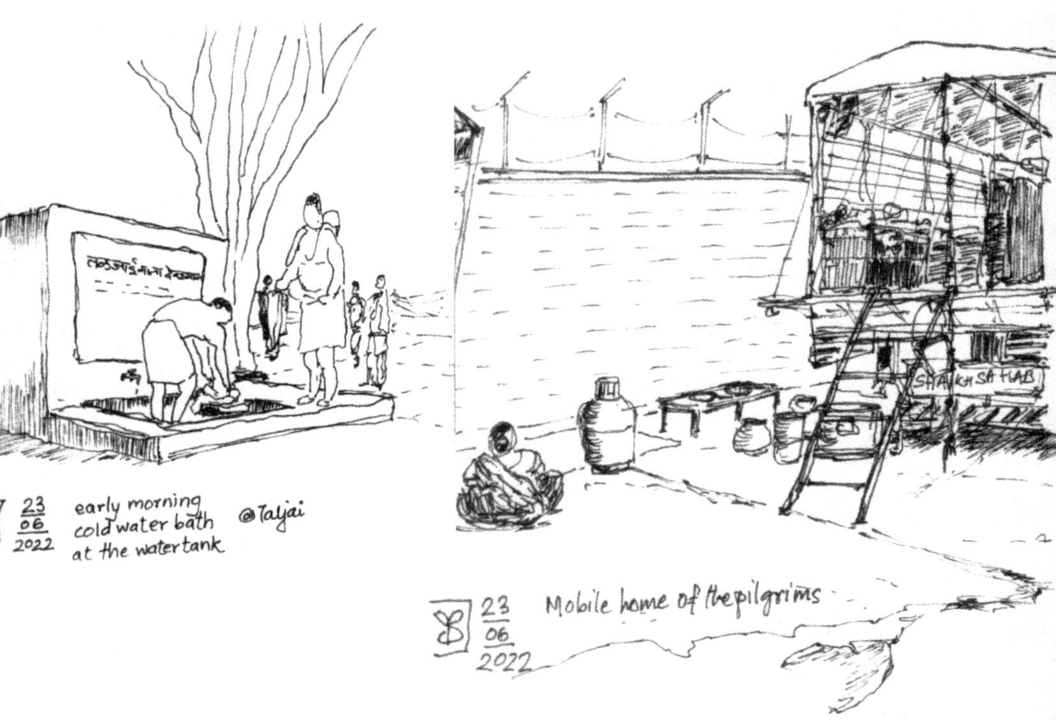

23
06
2022
early morning
cold water bath   @ Taljai
at the water tank

23
06
2022
Mobile home of the pilgrims

MahaForest

The Maharashtra Forest Dept has been quite busy here in the past few years and we have been seeing lots of earth moving equipment and excellent work of plantations and development being undertaken at the Panchgaon Parvati (Taljai) Forest Reserve. All visitors highly appreciate their excellent work.

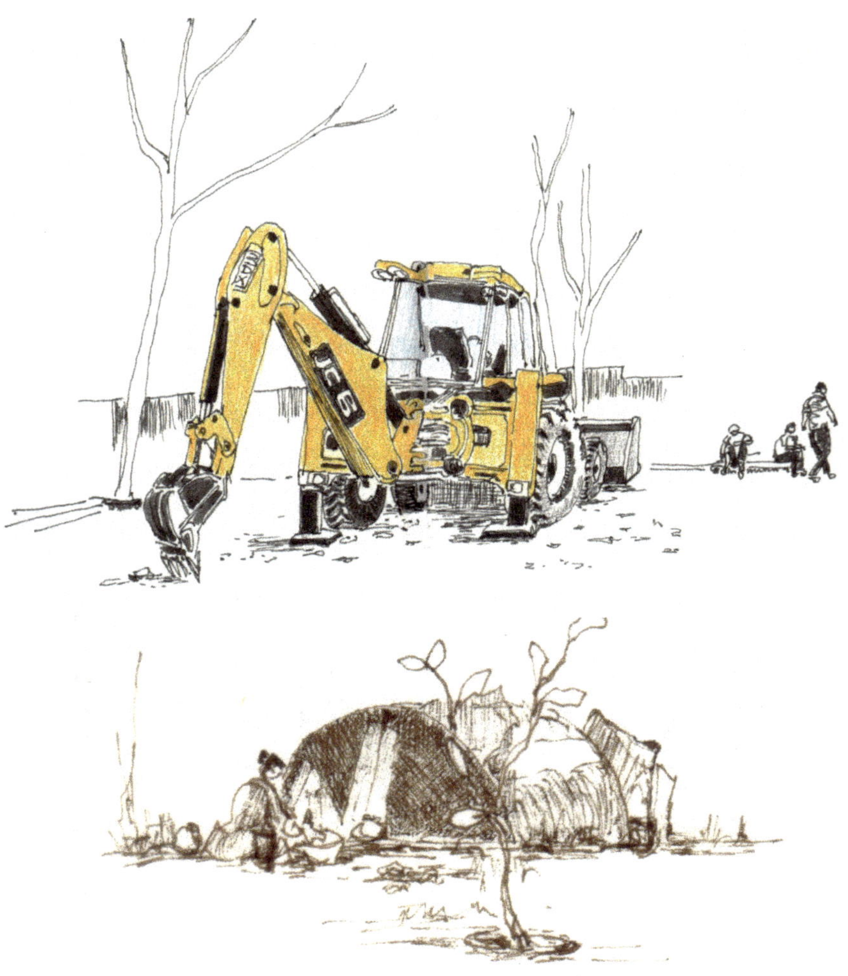

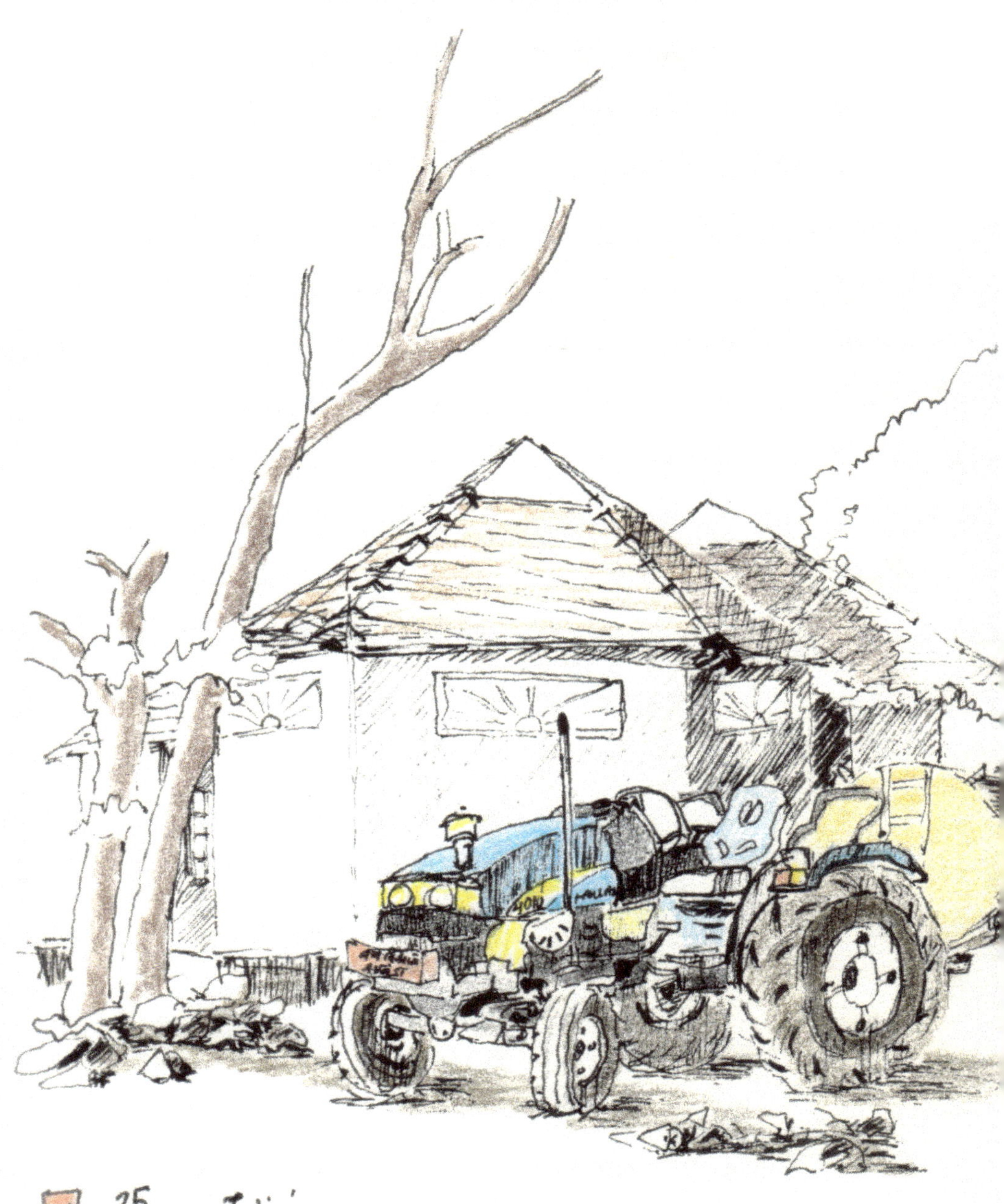

25
05
2022
@Taljai

Several of my Pune Urban Sketcher friends have also sketched at Taljai.

Gajanan Kurkute sketches great with a simple ballpoint pen. A few of his sketches of Taljai are seen below.

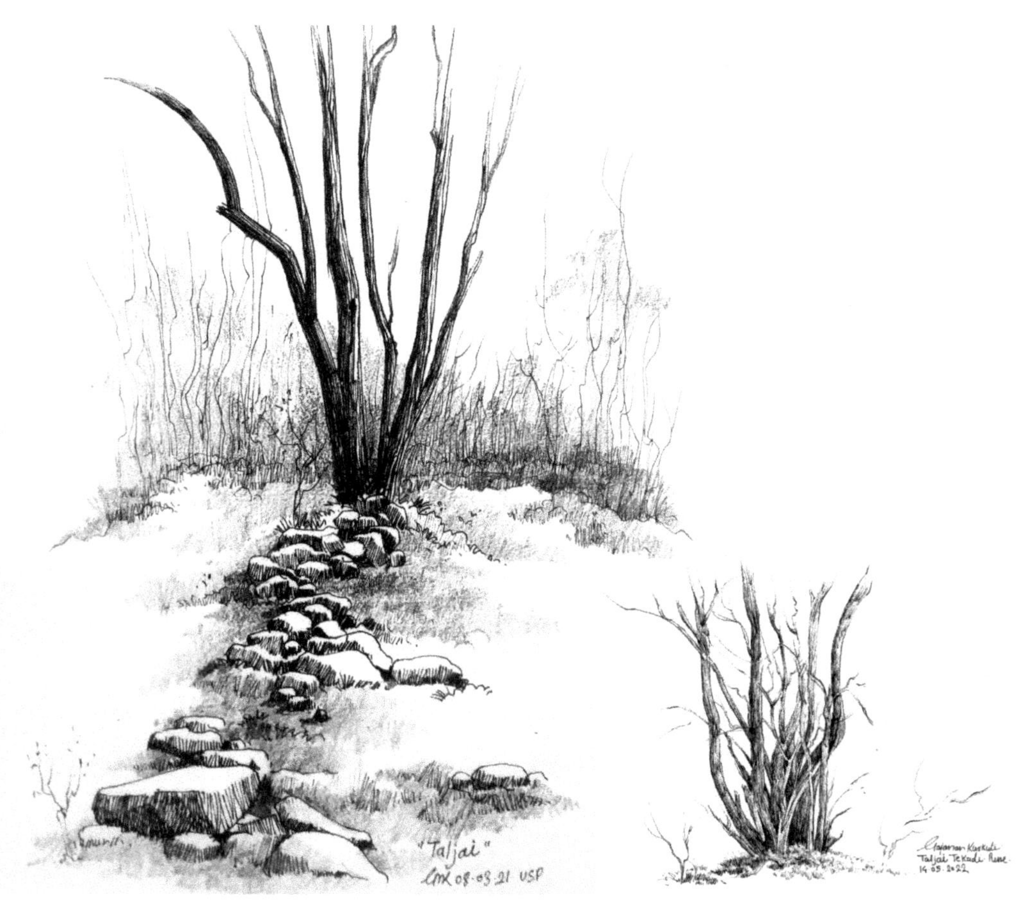

Manish Pimpley is a whiz at people sketching and some of
his sketches at Taljai are shown below

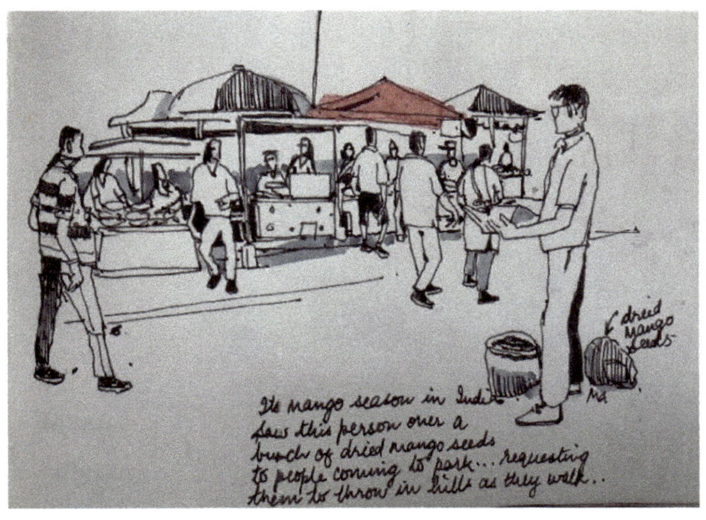

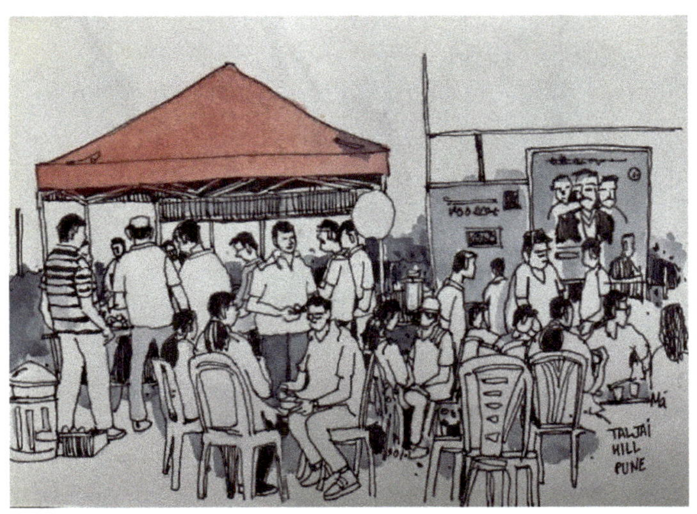

Prafulla Hudekar, an expert mariner is great with watercolors

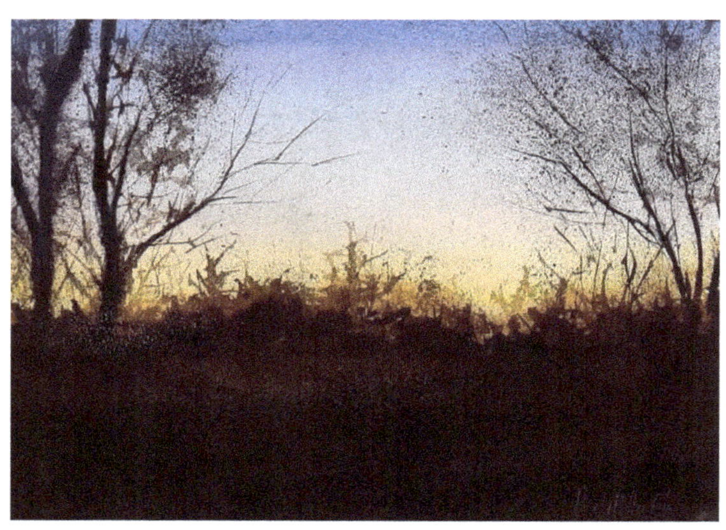

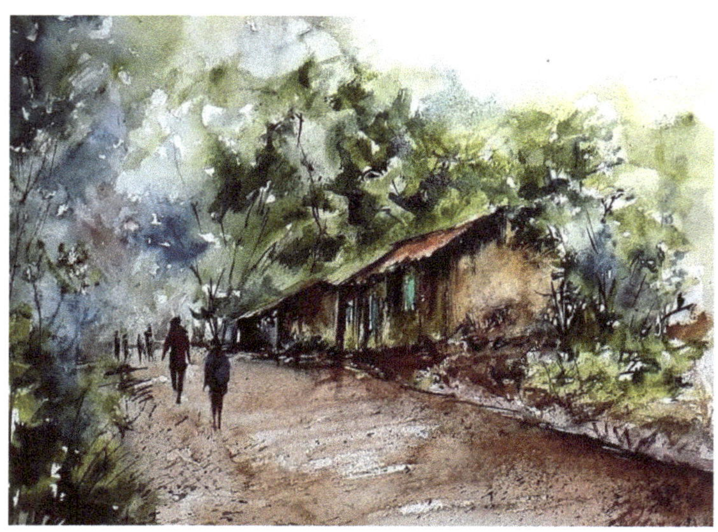

Acknowledgements

This book would not have been possible without the encouragement, guidance, and assistance of so many of my friends.

The germ of the idea to author a book came from Shirish Deshpande, who has authored several books about sketching. The idea of authoring a book on Taljai, came from Ar. Sanjeev Joshi, the founder of Urban Sketchers, Pune and from my nephews – Shyam and Shivaji, who have patiently waited while I suddenly stopped and started sketching in the middle of the walk in the forest. Their suggestions, appreciation, and criticism, all drive my sketching at Taljai.

Special thanks to Federica, Bettina, Paul, Rekha, and Shrish for reviewing the craft of this book and giving their valuable inputs and to Gajanan, who did the entire design of this book so beautifully.

My thanks also to Dr. Vinaybala Mehta and Ar. Sanjeev Joshi for their foreword for this book.

Last but not the least, divine grace guides all our efforts, and I am sure the goddess at Taljai Mata Devi Mandir blessed this small initiative, of the forest named after her.

About the Author

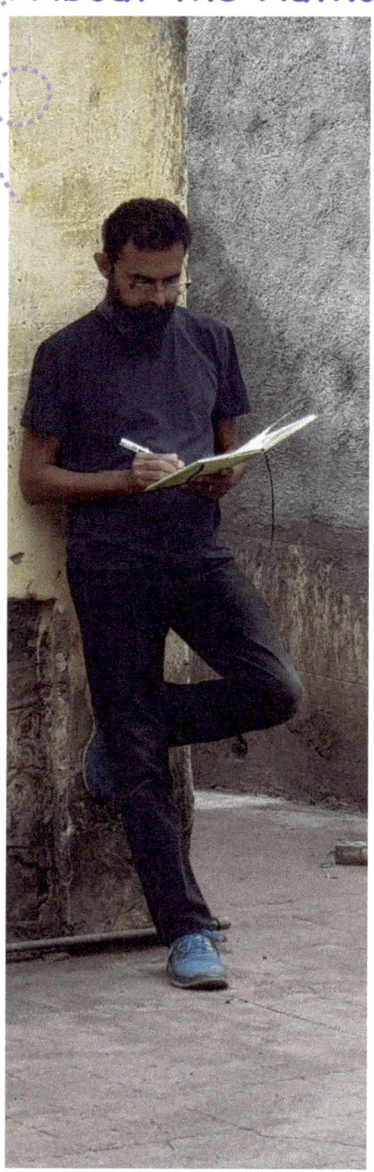

Subhash is an avid urban sketcher and a perennial student. Curious and eager to learn new things, he started sketching on approaching the age of sixty. He has gone about it in his usual way, absorbing learnings from those around him, searching for anyone who can teach him to do some part of it better, and having a lot of fun while going about it.

Sketching provides a wonderful counterpoint to his work as a Chartered Accountant, Lawyer, Business Consultant, Company Director, Trustee, etc.

Subhash lives in Pune with his family and connected with his large and diverse friend circle in Pune and around the world. He has served on the Board of Directors of companies such as Ambuja Cement Eastern Ltd, BPL Ltd, Karnataka Soaps & Detergents Ltd, amongst others. He has also served on the Boards of educational institutes such as the AISSMS and SSMS, which run schools and colleges, been a member of the Senate of the Poona University, Trustee of the Bhartiya Samaj Seva Kendra as Trustee of Shri Devdeveshwar Sansthan, which manages the historical properties of Sarasbaug Ganapati temple, Parvati temple complex, etc.

Instagram: subhash.usp

* 9 7 8 9 3 5 7 8 0 4 6 4 6 *